A Visit to Spain

1862

HANS CHRISTIAN ANDERSEN

A Visit to Spain
and North Africa
1862

TRANSLATED FROM THE DANISH
WITH AN INTRODUCTION AND NOTES BY
GRACE THORNTON

PETER OWEN · LONDON

ISBN 0 7206 0323 4

Translated from the Danish
I Spanien

UNESCO COLLECTION OF REPRESENTATIVE WORKS
This volume has been accepted in the
Translation Series of Danish Works
jointly sponsored by Unesco and the Danish
National Commission for Unesco.

For Signe

PETER OWEN LIMITED
20 Holland Park Avenue London W11 3QU

First British Commonwealth edition 1975
English translation © 1975 Peter Owen Limited and Grace Thornton

Printed in Great Britain by
Bristol Typesetting Co Limited
Barton Manor St Philips Bristol

CONTENTS

LIST OF ILLUSTRATIONS

Illustrations 1 and 2 and the sketch on p. 118 are reproduced by kind permission of Dr Niels Oxenvad, Odense Bys Museer; 3, 4, 5, 7, 8, 10 and 11 by permission of the Spanish National Tourist Office; 6 by courtesy of the National Portrait Gallery, London; 9 by courtesy of the Royal Academy of Arts, London. The cartoon on p. 73 is reproduced by permission of the University Library, Copenhagen.

FOREWORD

This translation of Hans Christian Andersen's *I Spanien* (rendered
here as *A Visit to Spain*) is based on the text of the edition published
in Copenhagen in 1971, with reference to the scholarly edition of
1944 published under the auspices of *Det Danske Sprog-og Litteraturselskab.*

I have taken the liberty of omitting all the verses with which the
text is interwoven. Some cuts have also been made in the more
repetitive prose passages, but I hope that these have been achieved
without a great loss, or detriment to the work as a whole. It is an
attractive account of a journey in Spain which has a deservedly
high place in the Andersen canon.

For permission once again to take advantage of his scholarship I
would make humble and grateful acknowledgement to Professor
Helge Topsøe-Jensen, director of the 1944 edition of *I Spanien*,
editor of the Collin and Henriques correspondence and of Andersen's autobiography and last, but by no means least, editor-in-chief
and indeed the inspiration of the long-awaited edition of the Andersen Journals. The Royal Photographic Society identified the 'famous
photographer' whom Andersen saw in the *Alhambra*; the Royal
Academy produced details of John Phillip and his copy of the
Velasquez masterpiece; John Townsend of University College
Library, London, found copies of Washington Irving's *Alhambra*
and of some of Andersen's early works : to them my thanks and to
Oleg Polunin for his botanical advice.

Esther Heilbuth in the British Embassy, Copenhagen, and John
Muir, the British Council representative in Madrid, have shown
exemplary patience in dealing with my pleas for help, as have other
former colleagues in Spain and Tangier.

use of her *Life of Hans Christian Andersen* (1933), but above all, I owe to Ellen Jørgensen most of such knowledge of Danish and the Danes as I can reasonably claim.

London, 1973-4   Grace Thornton

INTRODUCTION

'The land of enchantment beyond the high Pyrenees' is how, in a poem in 1838, Hans Christian Andersen described Spain, a country to which he had felt himself drawn since early childhood.

In his autobiography *The Story of my Life* (*Mig Eget Eventyr Uden Digtning*) he says :

> . . . what particularly impressed itself on my memory, and was continually refreshed by later re-telling, was the Spaniards' stay in Fyn in 1808 : although I was not more than three years old at the time, I can still clearly remember the dark-skinned foreigners, the noise they made in the streets and the sound of cannon shot. I remember that I saw them sleeping on straw in the old half-ruined church by the hospital and one day a Spanish soldier took me in his arms and pressed to my lips a silver medallion he had round his neck. I remember that my mother was angry – she said there was something Catholic about this, but I liked the picture and the strange man who danced me up and down, kissed me and wept – he surely had children himself at home in Spain.*

Two of his early short plays, *Spanierne i Odense* (The Spaniards in Odense) and *25 Aar Derefter* (25 Years Later), together called *Skilles og Mødes* (Parting and Meeting) and produced at the Royal Theatre in Copenhagen in 1836, had as their subject the effect of the Spanish soldiers on the susceptible hearts of the young ladies of Odense, and his full-length verse drama *Maurerpigen* (The Moorish Maid), 1840, dealt, albeit conventionally, with the romance and tragedy of the conflict between the Moorish Power and Christian Spain.

*'See Chapters IV and IX below.'

1

Andersen planned to go on to Spain from Italy in 1846 and sailed from Naples to Marseilles, from there making his way via Perpignan to the frontier. But he found the heat too much for him and decided that the further journey was not worth the effort just for a few days in Barcelona. 'I stand,' he said, 'like Moses and look over to the promised land, on which I shall not set foot. But, God willing, one winter I will fly here again from the north, into that rich, beautiful land from which the sun with its flaming sword now excludes me.'

In 1860 he thought once again of going there, this time from Switzerland, but it was almost as if he was hesitant to test the reality of his imagining – this time he made his lack of knowledge of Spanish and a reported outbreak of cholera the excuse to stay well on the northern side of the Alps.

But at last, in 1862, he made definite plans to visit Spain and this time did so, spending in all nearly four months travelling by coach, train and coastal steamer, taking in en route Gibraltar and a visit to Tangier.

Andersen always did his homework before he visited a new country. There was little available in Danish about Spain, other than Christian Molbech's *En Maaned i Spanien*, 1848, which he may already have used for the Spanish background piece in his *Historie fra Klitterne* (A Story from the Sandhills) in 1859. He knew Herder's *Der Cid* and a German version of Cervantes. C. C. Plüer's *Reisen durch Spanien*, 1758, provided him with the Moorish stories and legends which he uses in his chapters on Granada and Toledo, and Edvard Brinkmeier's survey of modern Spanish literature, published in Göttingen, 1850, gave him the factual background to the writings and careers of the Spanish writers he met in Madrid.

As a guide for routes, hotels and so on during his actual journey, Andersen used F.W. Hackländer's *Ein Winter in Spanien*, 1855, and in his Journal he mentions a French guide book, the *Guide-Joanne*, published by Hachette in 1850, which he seems to have had with him.

In his library at his death there were also two English books – *Italy, Spain and Portugal* (London, 1840) and *The Traveller's Handbook for Gibraltar* (1844), together with two Spanish phrase-books, *Der Kleine Spanier* (1843) and *Habla v. Castellano?* (1856). It may well have been from these two latter books that he acquired his 'treasury of Spanish words'.

He was therefore as well-informed as could reasonably have been expected and with this knowledge – and perhaps a touch of complacency in that he could already describe himself as a writer on Spain – he set off from Copenhagen, taking with him young Jonas Collin, who had been his companion on a visit to Italy the year before.

Jonas was the grandson of old Jonas Collin who, as the Financial Director of the Royal Theatre in Copenhagen, one of the King's Counsellors and Secretary of the *Fondem ad Usos Publicos*, had, some forty years before, been the young Hans Christian Andersen's chief benefactor. Not only did he get money for the boy, he also took him into the close-knit Collin family, where Andersen was ever after treated as an adopted son and brother. To his son Edvard, old Jonas had entrusted the especial care of his protegé. It was Edvard who generally managed Andersen's business affairs – and tidied up his ill-spelt manuscripts; after the father's death, it was to Edvard and his charming wife, Jette, that Anderson turned as his nearest 'family' : in their house he was at home.*

Young Jonas was their only son : he was studying zoology and apparently only got leave of absence for the long trip to Spain because he intended to do some scientific work there. He was serious, almost humourless, and seems to have inherited all the reserve and more conventional characteristics of the male Collins, with little or nothing of his mother's affectionate charm – she who, as Andersen once said, knew 'how to put sunshine into a letter'.

In his letters from Spain, Andersen contented himself with recording – sometimes with a certain wry humour that was certainly not lost on Jonas's parents – the young man's all too frequent bad temper, but his journal goes further and reveals his very genuine unhappiness during some of the visit. He wanted always to give and was now in a position to do so – and to whom better than one of the Collin family, with which he had always so much wanted to feel on completely equal terms. If only Jonas, whom he thought of as a

* See Hans Christian Andersen, *A Visit to Portugal 1866* (Peter Owen, 1972): Introduction and Appendix I.

favourite nephew or, indeed, as a younger brother, could have
brought himself not just to say thank you, but quite simply to show
signs of enjoyment, there is little doubt that the older man would
have responded with a glad heart – but graciousness does not seem
to have been part of Jonas's make-up. Of the two, the fifty-seven-
year-old writer was, in spirit, younger than the twenty-two-year-old
student, and there is something rather pathetic in the picture of
Andersen, as described in his journal, wandering restlessly alone
while Jonas either stayed in his room, pleading a headache, or clambered about on the rocks looking for 'specimens'.

In his heart of hearts Jonas may well have resented being under
any obligation to a man who, he perhaps thought, in one sense owed
everything to *his* family. And yet, abroad, there was no denying
that Hans Christian Andersen was a famous figure – he almost *was*
Denmark – with an easy, well-nigh automatic entrée into official,
diplomatic and literary circles where the name of Collin was un-
known.

Both Andersen and Jonas were avid for letters from the family,
who were at that moment on holiday in Italy. The postal services to
Spain were erratic and at every stop the first visit was to the Danish
consulate (where there was one) and the local post office. It is not
difficult to imagine the young man's reaction to his mother's suggestion, in a letter of 29 November 1862 to Andersen from Rome :
'Will you allow us to address Jonas's letters to you? In that way
they will surely be handled with care and be safer.'

At the same time, it is very likely that Jonas was often embarrassed
by Andersen's child-like enthusiasms, which he did not and neither
would nor could pretend to share. And, to be fair, Andersen was not
the easiest of companions : he was a nervous traveller and con-
spicuous by his tall gawky figure. It is clear that the Spaniards were
not always polite to foreigners and poor Andersen notes in his
journal the relief he felt in Granada on one occasion that he was
alone, when some soldiers and women on a balcony were obviously
laughing at him – and Jonas was *not* there to see. If Jonas had kept
a diary it might be instructive – but after all, he had travelled with
Andersen before and was, indeed, to do so again in 1870 when they
went to the Riviera together.

Hans Christian Andersen was an intensely personal and subjective writer : most of his stories in one way or another portray himself and his own feelings. But in his travel books he achieves rather more objectivity while, at the same time, always giving his own personal view of people and places. It is a measure of this skill that, in his book on Spain, there is little hint of the darker moods revealed in his journal.

It was of course his intention to write a book about this visit : he felt a duty towards his public who expected it of him. As a fore-taste, some of his letters from Spain were printed as soon as they were received in Denmark, as were some of his verses. After his return at the end of March 1863, he set about preparing the book for publication. He read some of the chapters, as they were com-pleted, to his friends, including the Drummond Hays, who were on leave in Denmark from Tangier. He read to them, of course, the chapter about his visit to Africa (Chapter XI) and 'felt himself much moved by its ending'. It was, incidentally, this chapter that was particularly mentioned in a *Spectator* review of 26 February 1864.

Part of this same chapter won much applause when read at the Students' Union in Copenhagen, together with descriptions of the bullfights, of Elche and the crinoline in Valencia. Andersen seems to have borne the students no ill-will for the obvious glee with which their paper *Sværmere*, in April 1863, had printed a cartoon of him with the chestnut seller in Málaga (see illustration p. 73).

I Spanien appeared in November 1863 as Volume 24 of Ander-sen's Collected Works. Its immediate reception was somewhat spoilt by the death on 15 November of King Frederik VII, but the reviews, when they did appear, were good.

In Denmark the book was reprinted in 1878 (after Andersen's death) and then not again, I think, until 1944 and 1971. Mrs Anne Bushby's English translation was published by Bentley in London in 1864 and various editions of *In Spain and a Visit to Portugal* were published in New York and Boston between 1870 and 1881, since when – so far as I am aware – no English translation has been made. An anonymous German translation appeared in 1864 but the book has apparently never been done in Spanish. (It was only in 1879 that the first selection of Andersen's stories appeared in Spain, but single stories may have been translated and printed earlier, as he suggests in Chapter XVI.)

There are, in the journal and letters from Spain, some items that one would like to have seen included in the book : it seems odd – at least to us I think – that Andersen omitted all mention of the Chapel of the Catholic Kings in Granada Cathedral, although he certainly visited it. He noted, but did not further use, the scene of two gypsies in prison who sat and gossipped through the barred window, with a basket hanging down on a rope outside for food and other offerings. In Madrid he was at the opening of the *Cortes* by the Queen, whom he saw some days later with her Consort at the Opera, 'wearing blue silk and a wreath of roses in her hair'. But perhaps it was for the sake of peace with Jonas that he did not tell in his book the story of the skirmish in Valencia with the Customs, who impounded all the bottles of spirit that Jonas had brought with him for his zoological specimens. However, he could not use everything that he had seen and heard, and what we have is rich enough. Indeed, some Andersen scholars would regard this as his best travel book : without doubt it is among the best.

As a milestone in Andersen's life of travel, the visit to Spain did not lead to very much literary work other than this book. In 1865 he wrote a three-act revised version of his early short play (*Spanierne i Odense*) called *Da Spanierne Var Her* : it had a short run at the Royal Theatre but was not a success and, indeed, did not deserve to be. The few factual insertions about Spain – as compared with the earlier work – only make it seem the more laboured and it is perhaps significant that the only Spanish character in the play, called rather oddly *Don Kuan*, never appears – his voice alone is heard, singing off-stage. Only one story, *Thepotten* (the Tea Pot) came out of the journey, inspired by a shard he saw in the garden of the hotel in Toledo, but it does not have a Spanish setting.

When he at last got to Spain, Hans Christian Andersen was, by the standards of the day, a fairly old man : he had lost much of the youthful exuberance that shines so clearly through some of his earlier travel books and it was not, in any way, an easy journey. The physical difficulties were not inconsiderable and Spain was still, in many ways, a closed country – certainly not yet used to foreign tourists. He did not find anywhere there the Danish circles that made life pleasant and easy in Rome and Paris, and linguistic problems must often have been both tiresome and tiring – hence the obvious relief of the welcome the travellers found in Tangier.

But he was a skilled and sensitive observer and although he did not have the breadth of knowledge—or the prejudices, be it said – of a Richard Ford or the missionary zeal of a George Borrow, his book can stand firmly on its own merits as a picture of Spain in 1862, a picture that is not wholly unrecognisable today.

G. T.

CALENDAR OF VISIT, 1862

23 July	Left Copenhagen with Jonas Collin for Germany, Switzerland and France en route for Spain. (Spent August in Switzerland with the Collin family)
30 August	From Montreux to Lyons
4 – 5 September	Perpignan, leaving early morning of 5 September for
6 September	Spanish Frontier, via La Junquera, Figueras, Báscara, Mediña, Gerona : by train from Gerona to Barcelona on night of 6 September
7 – 16 September	Barcelona
16 September	By night steamer to Valencia
17 – 19 September	Valencia
20 September	By early morning train via Almansa to Alicante, arriving late evening
21 – 22 September	Alicante
23 September	From Alicante by early morning diligence via Elche, Orihuela, to Murcia
23 – 26 September	Murcia
26 September	From Murcia by afternoon diligence to Cartagena
26 – 29 September	Cartagena
29 September	By afternoon steamer to Málaga, arriving morning of 30 September
30 September – 5 October	Málaga
5 October	From Málaga by evening diligence via Loja, Santafé, to Granada, arriving morning of 6 October

6 – 21 October	Granada (From 15 October staying near the *Alhambra* at *Fonda de los Siete Suelos*)
21 October	From Granada by evening diligence via Loja back to Málaga, arriving early morning of 22 October
22 – 29 October	Málaga, leaving by steamer on evening of 29 October for Gibraltar, arriving early morning of 30 October
30 October – 2 November	Gibraltar, leaving by steamer early morning of 2 November for Tangier
2 – 9 November	Tangier, leaving by steamer on evening of 9th for Cadiz, arriving morning of 10 November
10 – 13 November	Cadiz, leaving by train on afternoon of 13 November via Jerez for Seville
13 – 22 November	Seville, leaving by train on evening of 22 November for Córdoba
22 – 25 November	Córdoba
25 November	By diligence, early morning, via Andujar, Bailen, La Carolina (early morning of 26 November) to
26 November	Santa Cruz de Mudela, and on by train to Madrid (about midnight)
26 November – 2 December	Madrid : by morning train on 2 December via Aranjuez to Toledo
2 – 7 December	Toledo, returning to Madrid by train on 7 December
7 – 19 December	Madrid, leaving by train on 19 December for the *Escorial*, thence by evening diligence on 19 December to San Chidrián, and from there on by train, arriving midnight at Burgos
20 – 22 December	Burgos
22 December	From Burgos by train to Vitoria and Olazagutía, thence by diligence through the night to

23 December	San Sebastian, the Frontier at Irun Behobie and on to Bayonne
23 – 27 December	Bayonne
27 – 29 December	Biarritz

(Night of 29 December at Dax, then on to Bordeaux, 30 December – 14 January, 1863. Returned to Copenhagen via Paris and Germany on 31 March 1863)

A Visit to Spain

and North Africa
1862

I

Entry Into Spain

When railways were first opened in Europe the cry went up that this was the end of the good old ways of travel, that the poetry of travel had vanished, its enchantment lost. In fact it was at precisely that moment that the enchantment began. We now fly on wings of steam, and before us and around us picture follows picture in rich succession : like bouquets, there are cast to us now a wood, now a town, now hills and dales. We can get out and linger with what is beautiful, fly past what is dull, with the speed of a bird reach our destination—is this not magic? . . .

We had travelled over Germany, through Switzerland and into France. I was on my way to Spain, a beautiful country, but up to now seldom visited.

In France the railway came to an end at Perpignan; from there it is only a few hours' journey to the Spanish frontier but of this journey I had heard the most terrifying accounts. The diligences were described as torture-boxes, great heavy omnibuses with an entrance on one side only, so that there was no escape if the coach overturned – and they always overturned. Protestants in this land were said to be despised and persecuted as heathens; travellers were constantly exposed to attacks from bandits, and as to food – it was inedible. All this I had heard, all this I had read – and now I was on my way to experience it for myself. At Perpignan, I had to revert to the travel of olden days, again to take my seat in the poetical conveyance of our poetic old times. I am not poet enough to enjoy going back to the past, I prefer the present with all the blessings of modern life. But I was obliged now to go back in time – there was nothing else to do.

The diligence was due to leave at three o'clock in the morning.

To start at three o'clock means getting up at two o'clock, which means that one might just as well not go to bed at all, but nevertheless I lay down and slept a little in snatches, at intervals getting up to look at my watch and the starry skies. At half-past two I roused the servants, who should before that have called me, and after a drink of cold water – which was all one could get at that hour – my travelling companion Jonas Collin[1] and I made our way to the coach station, a great dark room like a stable, in a narrow street. A lantern standing on a barrel revealed six coaches huddled up together. There was not much room for all the passengers who were leaving from here. Now one traveller arrived, now another, none knew another, no one spoke to another; one sat down on an upturned crate, another sat on a trunk, a third disappeared into the harness hanging by the wall and many more were lost to sight in the dark corners of the shed. The carriages, to each of which were harnessed twelve horses, their bells jingling,[2] were loaded up with goods and people : it was grand. I got a seat in a coupé with a mother and daughter, both Spanish and both wearing inadmissibly large crinolines. I felt as if I were sitting on the edge of a balloon that was being blown up.

The whip cracked and off we went, swinging from side to side in the narrow streets, out over drawbridges, through fortifications – a setting fit for a medieval drama. At last, the broad, open highway lay before us. The Señora slept, dreaming no doubt of her beautiful Spain. I too dreamt of Spain, dreamt with open eyes and wakeful thoughts, wondering what I was going to see. The daughter neither slept nor dreamt, but all her thoughts seemed to be locked in the little overnight bag or large knitting-bag which she had in her lap. Her thoughts were in that bag – she was forever lifting it up and moving it, and this irritated me now that I had got used to being squashed by the crinoline. What could there be in that bag – and what might there be on the other side of the Pyrenees? These two thoughts ran wrapped together in my mind.

A bright lamp in front of the carriage lit up the road and its border of pines and plane trees. A little further on, like exclamation marks, stood slender cypresses : they have been likened to

furled umbrellas and here in the cloudless, light air they seemed
to be saying, 'Now are the showers and rain storms over. You can
roll up your umbrella – you are flying into the summer land of
Spain.' The light of the lantern made the umbrellas – that is to
say the cypresses – glitter but did not reach further. Beyond them
the earth was without form and void : around our little boxed-in
world was chaos and dark mystery. Of what lay behind we knew
as little as I knew of what was in that bag beside me. But I could
well imagine that the most precious object therein was not money,
neither gold nor silver, not precious jewels or a piece of Parisian
finery to be smuggled over the frontier. No, a poet's eye penetrated the secrets of a common or garden work-bag and I saw
what was there – the photograph of a man, a good-looking man,
a good friend, from his well-kept hair down to the point of his
well-polished boots – a handsome picture, but doubtless in his
own person still more handsome. I irritated him, being so close
beside his lady-love and he revenged himself by means of that
enormous work-bag. First it struck me in the stomach, then it lay
on my chest as the girl shifted from one position to another, holding fast her treasure, while mother slept on, snoring gently as
sleepers do who have difficulty in breathing.

A great star in the east, out over the Mediterranean, shone so
wonderfully clear, that I was uncertain whether I saw a star or a
lighthouse. For a long time I had wanted to begin a conversation with the Spanish girl, to make use (for which I have a little
talent) of my treasury of Spanish words – nearly one hundred
useful expressions.

What a lighthouse was called in Spanish, I did not know, but
I did know the word for star, and so I began with what I knew,
'estrella'. The word fell like a spark and kindled the fire of conversation in the girl : her words gushed forth like water from a
fountain and I understood not one syllable of what she said. In
the dawn light I saw the sea and said 'El Mar' and off she went
again. 'Inglés?' she said, 'Danés', I replied, and a dialogue en-
sued, that is to say, I gave the cue and she spun out the thread of
the conversation. I said 'La poesia de la España, Cervantes,.
Calderon, Moreto!' I named but names and with each one her

eloquence increased so that Mama was awakened – to be told by her daughter that I had been most interesting on the subject of Spanish literature; but it was she who had done all the talking, for I could not.

An Alpine landscape, a majestic snow-clad mountain towered before us. The rising sun suddenly cast its rays on the white snow and the mountain top glowed like red-hot iron, the whole mountain-side flamed. As the sun rose higher and the glow faded from the snow, the distant valley, as dark as night, took on a red-violet hue. It was a wonderful sight, an overture in colours to the Spanish Drama that was about to begin.

The road became more and more steep and most of the passengers got out of the diligence. In the fresh morning air we walked a long way uphill between bare rocks – and before I was aware of it, we were out of France! The whip cracked, the carriage rolled on – what had become of the high Pyrenees?

We were in Spain at La Junquera, the Spanish frontier town. The customs examination, which we had been told would be inquisitorial and rough, we found mild and polite, although we still had to go through the old-fashioned fuss over visas – but the main object was clearly money. We drank our chocolate in the open street, the baggage was loaded again and the passengers squeezed into the carriage as before. The space seemed to have got smaller, the seats harder and the sun was in our eyes. Señora's work-bag annoyed me, the crinolines irritated me. We drove through pools and streams: there were few bridges and where there was one, the diligence went underneath it all the same. Water splashed up on all sides, the heavy coach rolled and bumped, but had no time to overturn; it kept on its ponderous way, like an elephant running a race.

In Figueras, we found luncheon waiting and, for the first time, all the travellers were able to see each other. There was a good-natured Englishman, who was described as a kind of gardener – he cultivated genius. I do not really know what this means, I am simply reporting what his companion, a cheerful Frenchman, said. The Englishman was rich: he had read somewhere that it was always among the poorest class of folk that people of potential

genius in art and science were born and he was now on the hunt
to find such phenomena, that he might lift them over the barriers
of adversity, set them in the great gardens of education and there
plant a tree that would bear witness to his discovery. If he saw
a shepherd-boy in the fields, hacking away at a stick, then immediately the boy was set to be a sculptor, destined to become a
Phidias before next Easter. If he saw a street urchin chalking on
a fence a figure that faintly resembled a human being, the boy
was put into an art school. If the washerwoman's son scribbled a
verse to the greengrocer's assistant, thanking him for an old waist-
coat that still had some wear in it, then the boy was a poet and
must be transplanted. It was all very charming – and complete
nonsense.

The table groaned with food : meat and fish, boiled and
roasted; it was an excellent meal – and this in Spain, where one
had been told that the food was inedible. The fruit was wonderful, the wine fiery – and I did not get a sauceboat tipped over me
or a platter of fish down my back, as is so often my fate! But I
did suffer from my Spanish neighbour's heavy work-bag, which
held her beau : it fell and grazed my shins. The bag was always
at variance with me, pushing and teasing me.

The meal over, we all got back in the carriage. There were
twelve fresh mules, their bells jangling and the *mayoral*, or coachman, was also new : he made good use of his whip. The new
zagal, or mule-boy, was a bundle of restless energy, darting about
like a will-o'-the-wisp, springing now up on the coach, then down
on to the road, running alongside the mules or behind them,
throwing clods of earth at those in front, always shouting his
'*Thiah*' and calling to each mule by name, *Gitana* and *Caballero*,
Masanasa and *Catalina*; he cursed them, he praised them in
whole long sentences, which the animals understood, but I did
not. The *mayoral* shouted with him '*Thiah, thiah*', and the coach
rolled and bumped and creaked – but all the same we certainly
made progress. The pace slackened only when we were approaching the little town of Báscara, where we had to cross the broad,
deep river Fluvia. There was a strong current and no bridge. A
diligence ahead of us was already floundering out in mid-stream,

another was standing on the bank. The passengers were getting out to walk a little way to find a ferry to take them over, leaving the goods-laden coach to try its luck in reaching the other side. Our *mayoral* decided that what would be, would be, and went on : not one of us expressed fear. I found the experience new and amusing and gave not a thought to the danger – which indeed we were in, as I heard later in Barcelona. At the very place where we crossed, another coach had, some time before, overturned in the water, and two passengers had been drowned.

Some peasants from Báscara came to our aid : none was wearing more than a jacket and in this costume they steered and led us. Some held on to the coach, some to the mules and in front of us went the pilot who knew the ford and showed the way. In the deepest place the water came up to their chests and inside the coach we had to lift up our feet to prevent them from getting wet, but all was well this time.

By late afternoon we had passed the little town of Mediña and were nearing Gerona; the traffic on the road became more and more lively, as if there was a festival or market in the town. We saw picturesque clothes and handsome people, the women vivacious, laughing and chattering, the men with coloured *mantas*, riding on mule-back, smoking their cigarettes which they all know how to roll. We entered the town by a very long bridge, which was so narrow that only one coach could cross over at a time. For that reason a number of bays had been built where carriages could pull in to wait until the way was clear. But a heavily loaded diligence seemed to be regarded as 'gentry' and everything else made way for it : even in the town in the long narrow streets, it seemed to me that most of the vehicles we met were trumpeted out of our way. We reached the railway station and were released from the confining, dust-laden coach. Now the train journey, modern magic, would begin again. It really did appear to be witchcraft to many an old Señora, who crossed herself before setting foot on the compartment steps and again before sitting down in this devilish horseless carriage.

How wonderful it was to sit here instead of in that diligence : the seats were soft, one could stretch one's legs and really have room to breathe. The railway was still something of a novelty here and a lot of people went to see the trains depart. There was a drunken man with a fine new umbrella, but he was not allowed to travel in the state he was in. The gendarmes removed him from the train and he was as cross as cross could be. Since he could not hit the soldiers he took it out of his new umbrella, banged it against the stone platform, broke it, murdered it, treating it as he would like to have treated those men – and thus relieved his temper.

Several priests, old and young, got into our compartment, all smoking cigarettes. The signal was given, the old ladies crossed themselves and off we went. The Pyrenees lay behind us and green woods spread fanwise in the landscape, which became flatter and flatter. Pine trees lifted their evergreen heads and the land looked like a wooded park, all the way to the Mediterranean, which we reached at sunset. It lay before us blue and endless, its long waves breaking in surf on the sands, close by the railway line. The moon rose slowly and hung shining bright in the clear southern air.

It was on 6 September that, as a child, I first came to Copenhagen; it was on 6 September many years later that I first went to Italy and now, on the same day of the same month, Spain opened before me. It just happened – chance, as we call it, would have it so. In Lyons I had to wait for a day for my trunk which had gone astray; in Perpignan I had to wait two days to get a seat in the diligence, and so 6 September was still my day.

I was in a foreign country yet felt myself at home. It was the sea that made everything seem familiar, the wonderful sea which rolled towards me here from the coast of Africa with the same swelling waves as the North Sea on Jutland's coast.

Station followed station, all the carriages were filled up and finally, well after ten o'clock in the evening, we got to Barcelona. The wooden arrival shed was crowded with people, most of whom had no business there. Trunks, boxes, carpet-bags were all thrown out together. The old custom, which we knew for far too long at home, whereby baggage was examined at every stage of one's journey, still prevails in Spain. In the shed there was tremendous pushing and shouting. Outside there were omnibuses enough lined up, waiting, some near the exit, others further away outside the railings : each one had its own porter, who grabbed a piece of luggage and galloped off with it to his own particular carriage – that a traveller would prefer to keep his baggage together was of no moment. Screaming and shouting, one ran with a trunk to one vehicle, another bore away a carpet-bag to a second and the wretched owner was forcibly pushed into a third, despite the fact that the carriages were all going different ways. It was a regular battle to keep one's belongings together : everyone argued and pushed – it was like pillage on a battlefield. Fortunately, I had a Danish friend, Herr Schierbeck, living in Barcelona and he helped us through the tumult of arrival : he managed to get our baggage on the top of a carriage and Collin and myself inside, but he had almost to use force and it was a miracle that we lost not one piece of luggage, nor indeed ourselves, in that confusion, noise and turmoil. But there we were safely in a carriage, which moved off creaking and swaying. Gas lamps glittered, broad streets opened on to palatial buildings and led to *La Rambla*, a busy promenade full of people. Shops were lit up and there was a lively bustle everywhere. We stopped at the hotel *Fonda del Oriente* where two rooms, each with bed and balcony, awaited us – and the supper table was laid.

The balcony door was open; it was busy and cheerful down there on the broad, tree-lined promenade. The sky above was incredibly clear, almost blue-green; the moon sailed like a gleaming ball through endless space. From side streets came the sound of castanets. I did not want to go to bed, but wanted the night to gallop away so that soon I could see by daylight this, to me, new, strange place, Barcelona, the capital of Catalonia.

II

Barcelona

Early in the morning I was awakened by music : a regiment of soldiers was marching up the *Rambla*. I was very soon down on the long avenue which divides the city in half, from the *Puerta del Mar*, the promenade along the sea-wall, to the *Puerta Isabel Segunda*, outside which is the railway station for Pamplona. It was not the time for a stroll, rather the hour for business. There was a bustle of folk from town and country, office and shop workers on foot, peasants on their mules, heavy wagons with heavy loads, light carriages with nothing, carts and omnibuses. There were cries and shouts, whips cracked, bells and bronze ornaments jingled on horses and mules; the noisy traffic wove in and out – one knew one was in a great city. The large cafés looked well-appointed, if rather ornate, and already the outside tables were full. Smart barbers' shops, their wide doors wide open, alternated with the cafés, and inside they were busy with lathering and shaving and hairdressing. Wooden stalls with oranges, pumpkins and melons were set out on the pavements, and here a house, there a church wall was hung with cheap pictures, with robber-stories, rhymes and ballads 'printed this year'. There was so much to see, where shall I begin, where shall I end, on *Rambla*, Barcelona's boulevard?

When I visited Turin for the first time last year, I had the feeling that I was in the Paris of Italy; here I felt that Barcelona was the Paris of Spain. There was a French air about the place. One of the narrow streets nearby was very crowded with people. Shop after shop was filled with a variety of things – *mantas*, *mantillas*, paper and ribbon fans flaunted their colours, glowing and tempting. I wandered where chance took me. The side-streets got narrower, the houses more shy of the sun – they were not fond of windows, but all had thick walls and awnings over the court-yards. I came to a little square : a trumpet sounded and people gathered round as some jugglers, clad in vests, coloured swim-ming-trunks and a conviction that they were artistes – born to perform under a theatre roof and not in the street – were spread-ing a carpet over the paving stones, about to display their talents. A little black-eyed child danced and shook a tambourine before being tumbled head over heels and almost tied into knots by its half-naked papa. In order to see better I mounted a couple of steps in the entrance to an old house with a single Moorish-style window and two horseshoe arches supported by slender marble columns. Behind me the door was half open : I looked in and saw a thick hedge of geraniums growing round a dust-dry fountain. An enormous vine overshadowed most of the place, which seemed forsaken and dead : wooden shutters hung on one hinge in loose window frames, as if ready to fall. Inside it looked as though the place were given over to bat-filled twilight.

I went on and turned into another street, even narrower and more crowded. I will call it Church Street because here, hidden away between tall houses is the Cathedral of Barcelona : it stands there unimpressive and without pomp, so that one could walk by it unaware. The crowd took me by the arm and propelled me through the little door and into an open arcade which, with altars on each side, led up to the church and to an orange grove, planted when a mosque had stood there. Water still splashed in the great marble basins where the Muslims used to wash their faces before and after prayers. In one basin there was a charming little bronze statue of a rider on horseback, standing out on a metal pipe, with water splashing up round the horse. Close by, goldfish glided about among juicy waterplants and behind the high trellis geese were swimming – I should have preferred to say swans, but one must stick to the truth if one wants to be original as a travel writer. A rider in a fountain and real geese did not seem to put one into the mood for prayer, but there was much else here to do so. Before the altars in the arcade people knelt in prayer and through the great open door of the cathedral came the smoke of incense, the sound of the organ and choir. I walked under the vast, vaulted roof : here was majesty and solemnity, but God's sun could not penetrate the painted windows : herein was a brooding twilight, deepened by smoke.

I felt weighed down. I felt a need to get out into that open cathedral whose roof was the heavens, where sunbeams played on the orange trees and rippling water : outside where the faithful knelt in prayer the soft full notes of the organ bore my thoughts upwards to God. This was my first church-going in Spain.

From the cathedral I went back through the same narrow street and into another just as narrow, but gleaming with gold and silver. In Barcelona and many other Spanish towns, the medieval custom still prevails whereby the different Guilds, for example the Shoemakers and Metalworkers and others, each have their own street where only their work is sold and where one has, therefore, their whole range of goods to choose from. I was now in the street of the Goldsmiths with shop after shop filled with golden neck-laces and beautiful jewellery.

In one of the side-streets they were demolishing a big old house: a stone staircase several storeys high hung rocking against the side of the wall; a great well with curious ornamentation was half hidden among stones and rubbish. It was the house of the Grand Inquisitor that was disappearing. The Inquisition itself has long since disappeared, just as in our day the monks have gone and the cloisters are deserted.

From the open square with elegant arcaded buildings, by the Queen's Palace one reaches the promenade along the sea-wall. The view from here is extensive : one can see the ancient *Mons Jovis* and pick out the yellow zigzag stripe of the road up to the Fort of Montjuich, that rises up proudly, hewn out of the rock on which it stands. There is the open sea, the harbour crowded with ships and the suburb of Barceloneta – and a noisy place that is.

The streets are right-angled, long and with only poor-looking, low houses. There are booths with clothing, counters with food, trash and rubbish everywhere. Carriers' carts, fourwheelers and mules weave in and out, half-naked children tumble about in the sun and dust. It is very crowded but there are bathing huts down on the beach where one can take a refreshing bathe.

B

Although the weather and indeed the water were still warm, they were already taking down the big wooden shed and only a fence remained as a screen against the busy highway. We had to wade over a stretch of sand to reach the surf and take a dip – but how salt and refreshing it was. I came out rejuvenated and got back with the appetite of a young man to the hotel, where an excellent meal was waiting. It was as if the host had set out to prove how untrue was the contention that there was no good cooking in Spain.

It was a beautiful evening and after dinner we joined the crowd, strolling along the *Rambla.* The men were very well coiffured and elegant, all smoking cigars; one even sported a monocle and looked as if he had been cut out of a French fashion magazine. Most of the ladies wore the becoming Spanish *mantilla,* the long, black, lace veil set over a comb on the top of the head and hanging down to the shoulders. In their delicate hands their spangled black fans fluttered gracefully. A few ladies were dressed in French fashion, with hat and shawl. On both sides of the avenue people sat in rows on stone benches or chairs under the trees, and at tables set right out in the street in front of the big cafés where every place was taken, both inside and out.

In no country have I seen such excellent cafés as in Spain. For elegance and taste, Paris is far behind. One of the most beautiful, where friends and I met daily on the *Rambla,* was lit with hundreds of gas lamps. The tastefully painted ceiling was supported by slender columns and the walls were hung with good pictures and mirrors. Galleries upstairs led to small apartments and billiard rooms. In the garden were flowering bushes and a fountain and over it stretched a large awning which was rolled back in the evening so that one could see the clear, blue-green sky. Frequently it was impossible to find a vacant table, either up or down, indoors or out : every place was taken. And people of all classes were to be seen there : elegant ladies and gentlemen, the military of all ranks, peasants in velvet jerkins, coloured *manta* slung over the arm. I saw one man, obviously of the poorer class, arrive with four small girls who gazed with curiosity, almost awe, at all the splendour around them. A visit to the café was obviously for them as great an event as the first visit to the theatre is for many other children. Although the place was crowded and everyone was engaged in lively conversation, the noise was never overwhelming : one was conscious only of a gentle murmur accompanied by a piano. In all the bigger restaurants in Spain, a man sits at a piano all the evening and plays one piece after another, but no one takes any notice – it is just background noise.

The *Rambla* became more and more animated; the seemingly endless avenue was transformed into a crowded, festive hall.

Social life as we know it, between families, does not exist here. People get to know each other in the fine evenings on the promenade. They go to the *Rambla* in order to sit together, to talk together, to enjoy each other's company and agree to meet again tomorrow. Acquaintance is struck up and the young make their assignations, but until a betrothal is formally announced they do not meet in each other's homes. It is on the *Rambla* that a young man finds his future wife.

The first day in Barcelona was rich and colourful and the succeeding days no less so. There was so much new to be seen, so much that was especially and genuinely Spanish, even though one was conscious of the French influence in a place so near to the border.

During my stay in Barcelona the two main theatres, the *Principal* and the *Teatro del Liceo*, were closed. Both are on the *Rambla*. The *Teatro del Liceo* is said to be the biggest in Spain. I saw it by daylight. The stage is very large indeed, very deep and high. I was there during a rehearsal of an operetta with jingling, ding-dong music, which the theatre-school and chorus were to present that evening in one of the suburban theatres.

The auditorium was tastefully decorated, the boxes much gilded, each having its own ante-room with velvet-covered sofas and chairs. In the centre, facing the stage, was the Director's box, from which went hidden telegraph-wires down to the stage : by pressing a button, orders could with lightning speed reach the prompter, the stage manager or any other assistant. A bust of the Queen stood in the vestibule at the foot of the beautiful marble staircase. The public foyer surpasses in its elegance anything of this kind that Paris has to offer, and from the balcony there is a magnificent view over Barcelona and the sea.

An Italian company were playing in the *Teatro del Circo*, but there, as in most Spanish theatres, nothing was given but translations, usually from French.

The most popular entertainment in Spain, which appeals to all classes, is the bullfight. Every town of any size has its *Plaza de Toros*, the largest I think being in Valencia. For nine months of the year this show is the regular Sunday entertainment. In Barcelona we were to go to a bullfight the following Sunday : we were told that there would only be a couple of young bulls and that it would not really be a proper fight, but nevertheless it would give us some idea of what went on.

From the *Rambla* one takes an omnibus or cab to the *Plaza de Toros*, a large, circular, stone building, which is some way out, not far from the Gerona railway station. The vast arena is covered with sand and enclosed by a wooden fence about twelve feet high, behind which there is a long open corridor for standing spectators. If the bull decides to jump over the barrier, they have no choice but to jump into the arena – and if the bull springs back there, then they must try to return to their places. Behind this open space, going all round the amphitheatre, is a stone gallery for the public and above that again are a couple of wooden galleries, divided into boxes with benches or chairs. We decided to remain down below in order to be in the middle of things. The sun was shining over part of the arena; bespangled fans rippled and glittered, looking like so many birds fluttering their bright wings. The building holds about fifteen thousand people; there were not that many here now, but it was comfortably full. We had been warned that at a bullfight there was a great deal of vulgar humour and free speech and we were advised to avoid drawing any attention to ourselves by, for example, anything in our dress, and thus risk being the butt of popular humour. Someone would decide to shout, 'Off with his fancy gloves! Off with his white city hat!'; witticisms would follow and the sport would be in full swing – there was no holding back, the noise increased, the will of the people prevailed – and off came gloves and hat willy nilly – if not with the wearer's co-operation, then by force.

As we entered the music was deafening, ear-shattering : people were shouting and screaming. It was like a wild carnival. Men pelted each other with bags of flour and sausages, and the ladies did not escape : here flew oranges, there a glove or an old hat, all with cheerful uproar. The glitter of the fluttering fans, the coloured *mantas* and the dazzling sunshine affected the eyes as much as the noise affected the ears : one felt as in a maelstrom of animation. Now the trumpets sounded a fanfare, one of the gates of the arena was opened and the cavalcade of bullfighters entered. First came two men in black clothes with large white cravats, each with staff in hand. They were followed by four *picadores* on old horses, their lower limbs well padded to prevent injury if the bull turned on them : they carried lances with which to defend themselves, but the padding made them quite helpless if they fell off their horses. Next came half a score of *banderilleros*, handsome young men dressed like Figaro in velvet and gold. After them, in silk embroidered with gold and silver, came the '*Espada*', his blood-red cape over his arm and in his hand the well-tempered sword with which he was to deal the death blow. The cavalcade ended with four mules, decked out with plumes, bronze ornaments, coloured tassels and jingling bells. At a gallop and to rousing music they would drag the slaughtered bull and any dead horses out of the arena.

The procession circled round and halted in front of the balcony where the Chief Magistrate was sitting. One of the two black-clad officers – I think they are called *alguaciles* – rode forward and asked permission for the performance to begin. The key to the door of the bull's stall was then thrown down to him. The wretched bulls are quartered immediately underneath part of the auditorium, and there they have spent the entire night and the morning without food or drink. From the mountains they have been led into the city yoked to two tame bulls; trustingly they have followed – to kill or be killed in the arena. But today they had themselves no bloody part to play : their horns had been padded to render them harmless. Only two were to fall to the

thrust of the *Espada*'s blade : the performance today, was, as we
had been told, not serious, and no real lover of bullfighting would
bother to attend. For this reason the show began with a comic
scene, a fight between the Moors and Spaniards in which, naturally, the former were portrayed as ridiculous, the latter as
doughty. A bull was let in, its horns so bandaged that it could not
kill, but if the worst came to the worst it could break a man's
ribs. There was much running and jumping about, fun and
laughter.

Then came the real fight. A very young bull rushed in and
came to an abrupt halt in the ring : it was dazzled by the sunlight, the coloured *mantas* and the movements of the crowd. The
wild shouts, the blasts of the trumpets and the blaring music came
upon it so unexpectedly that it obviously felt, like Jeppe[1] when
he awoke and found himself in the Baron's bed, 'What on earth
is this, what has happened to me?' Unlike Jeppe, it did not weep,
but thrust its horns down into the sand, its back legs showing their
strength as the sand whirled in the air. But that was all it did and
it seemed completely cowed by all the noise and wanted to get out
again. In vain did the *banderilleros* tease it with their red capes,
in vain the *picadores* brandished their lances, which they dare not
use until the animal attacks them. At real fights it can happen
that in a flash the bull will toss both horse and rider so that both
fall; when this happens the *banderilleros* must try to drive the
furious animal to the other side of the arena, while the horse is
pulled to its feet and the rider remounted for a new onslaught.
The horse has one eye covered so that it cannot look directly at
its adversary and take fright. Very often, at the first encounter,
the bull drives its pointed horn into the horse so that its entrails
spill out. They are pushed in again and the gash is stitched so
that the wretched beast can bear its rider for a few more minutes.
Today the bull just would not fight; a thousand voices shouted
'*El ferro!*' The *banderilleros* moved up with long darts to which
were affixed waving ribands and squibs, and when the bull advanced towards them they sprang aside and with practised dexter-
ity contrived each to thrust a dart into the bull's neck. The squibs
exploded, the darts burned, the beast was maddened and vainly

shook his neck and head. Blood streamed from his wounds. Now came the *Espada* to give the death-blow. The blade had to be aimed at one particular spot in the neck, but on this occasion it was several times mis-aimed or too lightly thrust. The bull rushed about with the blade in his neck; another thrust followed. Blood came out of the animal's mouth; the public hissed the clumsy *Espada*. Finally the blade went into the fatal spot and immediately the bull sank to the ground.

A resounding *'Viva!'* rose from a thousand throats, with the clang of trumpets and kettledrums. The mules with bells, banners and plumes went round the arena at a wild gallop, dragging the dead bull after them. The blood was covered with fresh sand and another bull, just as young as the first, was sent in, goaded on its way with a sharp iron spike, in order to excite it. In the beginning this bull was more aggressive than the first, but very soon it too got frightened. The public demanded fire: the darts, squib-pointed, were shot into its neck and soon it fell victim to the *Espada*'s blade. 'Do not think that this is a real Spanish bullfight,' said our neighbour to us. 'This is only child's play!' And with play it ended. The public were allowed – all who wished – to jump the barrier into the arena: old and young alike took part in this entertainment. Two bulls with well padded horns were driven in. There was much jumping and rushing about as the bulls themselves sprang with the public over the first barriers and joined the people who were still standing there. There were roars of laughter and shouts of hurrah until the Impresario, the manager for the day's contests, decided that enough was enough and ordered the two tame bulls to be sent in. The two fighters at once followed these back into their stall. Not a single horse had been killed, only the blood of two bulls had been shed. This, compared with normal practice, was regarded as nothing at all, but we had anyway seen how the whole thing was arranged and now knew how easily popular feeling could be enflamed.

It was here in the bullring in 1833 that the revolutionary movement started in Barcelona, after they had begun to murder the monks and to burn the monasteries in Saragossa. The mass of people in the arena started shooting at the soldiers, who returned the shots, and the revolution spread with fire and destruction through the land.

Near to the *Plaza de Toros* is the cemetery of Barcelona, only a short way from the open sea. Tall aloes form a fence and high walls enclose a town inhabited only by the dead. A gatekeeper and his family who are housed in the porter's lodge are the only living souls there. Inside there are long solitary pathways lined by six-storey, tenement-like houses in which, side-by-side, one on top of another, are walled cells, in each of which lies a corpse in his coffin. A large mortuary chapel with black-hung altars is the cathedral of this city of the dead; a grass plot with tall dark cypresses and a solitary free-standing monument afford some variety to these streets where the people of Barcelona, generation upon generation, dumb, silent inhabitants, rest in their death chambers.

The sun was scorching, penetrating between the white walls; it was so still, so solitary here that I felt depressed and anxious to get out into the land of the living. Only by the open gate to the highway could any sound of life be heard : it was the whistle of a locomotive. A train roared by and when the noise died away, one could hear the sound of breakers on the nearby shore. I made my way there.

Some fishermen were just landing their catch : wonderful fish, red, gold and blue-green, played in the nets. Naked dark-brown children were running about on the beach; dirty women – I think they were gypsies – sat and mended old clothes, their hair greasy, black, their eyes yet more black. The youngest had an enormous red flower in her hair and her teeth were as shining white as a Moor's. It was a group to paint on canvas. The City of the Dead was for a photographer – and one shot would have been enough because from whatever angle one looked the view was the same – the houses of the dead, one after another, all alike, with here and there a few cypresses like *crêpe*-decked, furled banners.

Towards the end of my stay in Barcelona it had rained very heavily during the night and was still raining the next morning when I went to the bank. There was not sufficient outlet and the water was over my galoshes. I got back wet through and while I was changing my clothes, the news came in that the *Rambla* was flooded and the water still rising. I heard people shouting and running. I went to the balcony and saw gravel being shovelled up in heaps in front of the hotel. On each side of the raised promenade there was a brownish stream of water and the paved part of the *Rambla* was a rippling, rising river. I hurried down. The rain had more or less stopped but there was more damage to come. I witnessed a a terrible spectacle – the dreadful power of the water.

Up in the hills the rain had been so torrential that the little river which runs beside the highway and the railway line was soon overflowing. Apart from the sea, there had formerly been an outlet for flood-waters into the old moat of Barcelona. But last year the moat had been filled up with gravel and stone so that it could be used for building extensions to the city. This outlet was therefore blocked. The waters rushed on, the river rose ever higher, overflowed its banks and broke through every obstacle. Soon the railway line was under water, the highway buried, with every hedge broken, trees and aloes uprooted by the violent river which rushed in through the city gates and onwards on each side of the pavement foaming like a mill-race. It took with it stalls, goods, carts and barrels – everything it found on its way. Pumpkins, oranges, tables and chairs sailed away: even an unharnessed wagon filled with porcelain was carried some distance downstream. Inside the shops people were up to their waists in water. The strongest among them were trying to throw ropes out over the water to the trees on the higher parts of the *Rambla* so that the women had something to hold on to, while they were passing through the torrent. I saw one woman carried away by the current : two men sprang out after her and managed to bring her to land – unconscious. There were cries and lamentation, and it was just as bad in the narrow streets nearby as it was in the *Rambla*. The water gained momentum and roared as from a burst dam, surging in high waves, thrusting against the lower balconies. People tried to block doors and windows in an effort to break the impact so that the water, which otherwise could break up everything, entered the houses with somewhat less force.

They had tried to lift up the great stone drain covers on the bridge to provide another outlet but this was not much help and in fact was the cause of further disaster. I heard later that several people had been sucked into the holes and had disappeared in the depths below. Never have I seen the power of water so displayed. It was dreadful. It was already washing over the high-lying promenade: people were fleeing, crying and screaming. Balconies and roofs were crowded, trees and furniture floated in the streets. The gendarmes were very busy trying to help and to keep order and the water still seemed to be rising. They said that in the church by the *Rambla* the priests were singing mass, up to their waists in water.

After about an hour, the flood began to subside and the waters sank. People thronged into the side-streets to see the damage there. I followed, walking with difficulty through slippery, thick, yellow mud. Water was being baled out of windows and doors: one got dirty and smelly. Finally I managed to reach the square where Herr Schierbeck lived. He had no idea of the extent of the disaster. In all the years he had lived there, there had often been heavy storms, but they had never caused such flooding and up-heaval. We made our way through the streets deep in filthy, stinking mud. The *Rambla* was strewn with overturned booths, tables, wagons and carts. Outside the city gate, the work of destruction was even more serious. In many places the road was broken up and the water streamed through, making cataracts. There were rows of carriages waiting with people from the country, who had to get out and walk if they wanted to get into town. Planks from a nearby timber yard were strewn over the fields like giant spillikins. By roundabout ways, clambering over uprooted trees and strewn timbers, we got to the railway station, which looked like a beaver's lodge, half in water, half on land. It was a roofed-in lake and for some distance the lines were hidden by the muddy water. The way home was as difficult as the walk out had been. We had to jump in and crawl out of holes in the sodden earth. Roads and paths were cut up by fresh streams. We waded through deep mud and got back to Barcelona coated with it. Never before had I had any idea of the power of a mountain river. . . .

I had already been in Barcelona for a fortnight and felt at home there. 'Now to Valencia,'[2] I said, and the thought of that lovely province was like the music of Weber. I wanted to travel by diligence : the journey by steamer along the coast had been described as most unpleasant, the ships dirty and not equipped for passenger comfort. If the weather was bad then it was very difficult indeed to get ashore : the ferries did not go into harbour so that the passengers had to jump down into a rocking boat on the open sea, and the weather could be so bad that these boats would not venture out to pick up passengers. We were already in mid-September and the calm weather was over. There had been a very strong wind during the last few days, with high seas breaking on the walls of the harbour. By diligence one would see something of the country and I would rather have travelled that way, but Schierbeck, and everyone else I consulted, were adamant in advising me against it. It was a long and difficult journey and the heat in the overcrowded diligence would be suffocating; moreover the roads were in shocking condition and one risked stopping at several places where there was no inn of any kind – perhaps, indeed, not even a roof for a night's shelter. The diligence from Madrid was two days behind schedule; already I knew about the lack of bridges in this country and how one had to cross rivers. But now I had seen in Barcelona itself the power and destructive force of a mountain stream. To travel by diligence was, for the moment, to expose oneself to great inconvenience, possibly, indeed to endanger one's life. There was a particular spot on the road between Barcelona and Valencia where the mountain stream very often took command and where more than once accidents had taken place. Only a few years ago an overcrowded diligence had completely disappeared there and it was thought that it had been carried away by the rushing torrent to the open sea, the Mediterranean.

Up to a few hours before the steamer was due to leave, I was still wavering as to whether I should go on it or take the diligence overland. Everyone advised the sea trip. The steamer which was going, the *Catalan*, was praised as one of the best and quickest : the engines were said to be good and the captain competent. I

decided on the sea trip. Herr Schierbeck and another friend came
to see us off. It was afternoon before the ship weighed anchor
and, rocking, made its way out to the open sea.

For some way out the water was still yellowish-brown from the
recent floods, but then suddenly the sea was clear and green
again. Barcelona lay stretched out in bright sunshine: the Fort
of Montjuich stood out clearly. The hills appeared to get higher
and over them all towered one still more lofty, curiously serrated
like the fins on the back of a fish – it was the sacred *Montserrat*
from where Loyola began a new life.[3]

III

Valencia

I love the sea[1] – that is to say, it must, when I am on it, stay calm, stretching itself out smooth and blue, a mirror for the heavens and for me. I love it when the storms do blow – that is to say, I love it thus when I am safely on dry land, otherwise it greatly upsets me.

On this occasion there was no storm but neither was it smooth and still. The wind was fresh and the ship rolled. I did not venture down into the saloon for dinner. My companion, Collin, felt fine : he even smoked a cigar after dinner and trustingly lay down in his bunk, while I sat up on deck in the wind as if I were in a swing. I do not much like that movement but there are a lot of things one does not like but has to put up with.

On the horizon were clouds, sharply outlined like mountains. In the evening sun they took on a dazzling red-gold colour. Soon a star twinkled in the high clear sky and more and more came out. It was a beautiful evening : one could see the whole of the hilly coastline, dark blue against the light sea. I did not sit alone. There was a young German from Mannheim on board who was going to Madrid and had elected to take the sea-route to Valencia since the railway was out of action between Barcelona and Saragossa. He was young and enthusiastic : he was delighted with the sea, which he had never known before, and delighted with the beautiful view of the coast. He expressed his feelings so naturally and frankly and when he heard who I was – and knew my works – I found myself at once with a young, happy travelling-companion who was all attention. He busied himself doing all he could to make me more comfortable – put his own woollen scarf round my neck and his cloak over my feet, because there was a cold breeze and the rolling of the ship prevented me from going down to my cabin to unpack. . . .

37

The wind began to die down and the sea grew calmer. It was fascinating to look down into the dark-blue water where, in the depths, shining fish glittered like precious stones or darting tongues of fire, like the flash of a sword-blade in the sun. The clouds assumed such shapes on the horizon that it looked as if there was land hard by. The foaming white waves glistened, their crests in the distance looking like long white buildings, appearing and disappearing. It was after ten o'clock when I went down to my cabin : I slept for part of the night watch. The sea was tolerably calm.

At daybreak I went out on deck again. Thick rain clouds hung over the sea to the north. The coast of Spain was high, bare and wild, and the distant mountains looked desolate and sombre. The sun came up : the clouds were shot through with gold and purple as it cast a violet-blue shadow over the dark hills, and the sea looked like blood-red oil. It was as if we were gliding over a smooth, transparent silk carpet, it was so clear and shining, and as the sun rose to full strength the wide expanse of sea was so motionless that we seemed to be sailing through space.

A number of dazzling white houses along the coast indicated that we were approaching a considerable town. The Roman Saguntum was pointed out to us on a hillside : of its enormous walls, towers and amphitheatres only low ruins now remain, overgrown with a wilderness of cacti. The town that has been built on top of all the old grandeur is called Murviedro. The Madrid-Valencia railway which is being extended to Barcelona has so far only been completed as far as this. From the ship we could see the train with its veil of smoke and long line of carriages moving along near the sea-shore. It would be some time yet before we reached Valencia. We were now at a village called Grao which is about two and a half miles from the city, to which we could go either by a later train or immediately by one of the many 'tartanas' which were waiting. These are two-wheeled carriages, each with a canopy against the sun : they are rather bigger than droskies, smaller than our bakers' carts but higher than these and upholstered with broad cushions. At the landing stage ragged, dark-brown urchins and wild-looking porters fell upon us. They pushed and fought, falling over each other in competition as to who should carry our bags to the customs house. A fellow passenger, a Spaniard whom we had met on board, took charge of us, got our baggage into one *tartana*, and ourselves into another, and off we went to Valencia. We drove through flat, fertile countryside which reminded me of Denmark : there were ditches on either side of the road, from which rose gnarled olive trees, rather like our willows among beds of reeds – but here the reeds were bamboos. The whitewashed cottages by the wayside had reed or straw thatches, as at home with us, and only the long, coloured curtains hung in the open doorways showed that we were in a southern land.

South of the ruins of Saguntum the land stretches out from the stony hills down to the sea. '*La Huerta*', the Garden, as the whole of the rich fruit and vine growing district round Valencia is called, is a very well cultivated area which, from Moorish times, has been irrigated by a network of bricked trenches. One sees deep wells, with a horse turning the wheel, tipping the water-filled jars into the trenches. Low, thick vines spread over the warm reddish earth. Lemon and orange trees are planted in small groves over which slender palms raise their sunshades.

A vast bridge, a dried-up river bed, ancient walls and a city gate of hewn stone blocks was our first sight of Valencia. Narrow, unpaved streets, with awnings stretching from house to house, led to a small square where a couple of empty diligences stood. We were at the *Fonda del Cid*.

The dark, twisting stairs and passages, the lofty, sparsely-furnished rooms, indeed everything about the place and service indicated that we were no longer in Frenchified Barcelona, but a good way into Spain. Luncheon was ready and the food was good : the grapes were as big as plums, fine and spicy to the taste, the melons melted on the tongue like snow, the wine was fiery and potent. The air was hot enough to bake us through. The big rush mats hanging over the open balcony doors in order to keep out the sun made little difference. The sun held sway. One sat on the balcony and gasped for air, which the ladies tried to capture with their fans. On each balcony sat a whole family, trying to get a breath of air. As soon as one stepped outside the window one was in society. Social life flowered up the walls, up from storey to storey. Down below, the square was deserted, the sun burned steadily and one felt no desire to go down and cast a shadow.

The bell rang for dinner and once again the table groaned with food. There was snail soup, tureens full of small snails still in their houses, in brown liquid – it was that in particular which looked so unappetising. Then there was squid, cooked in oil, but the following courses were edible and indeed very good.

The change from day to night was a sudden transformation. At one moment the clouds were sunlit and red, at the next, suddenly, the colours were quenched, the stars were out and it was dark down in the square. From a neighbouring house a light shone, reflected in the polished sign of a barber's shop. A young man came by strumming a guitar : he disappeared into a narrow street, but I could hear the guitar for some time and it put me into a Spanish humour – until a dog began to bark, another followed and soon the whole quarter was in the sort of uproar that I thought was to be heard only in Nyhavn² when one mongrel starts and all the ships' dogs join in to help with the concert. This was our first day in Valencia.

My wanderings in the town began early the next morning. The sun was already strong and it would be very hot indeed later on, as I knew from the previous day. We were in the middle of September and the warmth was almost unbearable – what would it be like here at the height of summer? It had rained during the night and there were big puddles in the muddy, unpaved streets. The square in front of the *fonda*, where the Archbishop's Palace also lies, was deep in mud which one had to jump over in order to reach a little lane where the cathedral lies hidden away. When he had conquered Valencia, the hero El Cid surveyed the city and surrounding district from the top of the cathedral tower. Most travellers begin their visit here with the same view, but I always prefer to get to know a place on the ground and then later, from higher ground, to pick out familiar landmarks.

I walked through the church and came out into a busy street which led to a big square, crowded with people and mules. They were mostly countryfolk, powerful-looking figures in picturesque costumes. They wear '*zaragüelles*', a kind of pantaloons reaching to their bare knees, and leather sandals laced round blue stockings, red belts and grass-green jackets with cross-lacing over their bare chests. Over the shoulder is thrown the decorative, striped *manta*. A scarf is wound round the head like a turban over which is a broad-brimmed hat. The whole effect is striking – but the reputation of these people is otherwise not good. It is said that they are very quick with the knife and they used always to be at odds with the townsfolk, who indeed look a different race, if their fair hair is anything to go by. The attacks and murders which not so very long ago were frequent occurrences in the town and district, were ascribed to these peasants, but now the Spanish Gendarmerie have enforced law and order and one can go out at night without any danger at all even in the most remote streets of Valencia. The women I saw were not as good-looking as in Barcelona. Some wore the long black *mantilla*, but most of them were wrapped up in bright yellow or flame-red shawls. There was a dazzling mixture of colour everywhere: each little stall displayed its most colourful wares and piled up on the ground were goods and vegetables such as enormous onions and bright green melons. Baskets full of common or garden small snails – like the ones we had had in the soup the day before – were on show in front of *La Lonja de la Seda*, the silk-mart, a most singular building with two colossal windows, each the size of a city gate. They gave light to a vast hall, the ceiling of which was supported by spiral columns, tall and slender as palm trees. Shining yellow silk lay in big rolls on the counters and floor.

From this lively part of the town I came to a quieter quarter, where a dozen or so men were sweeping the streets with brooms of flowering myrtle twigs. On both sides of the street were palatial houses, fountains and blossoming rose bushes in their courtyards. Striped awnings hung over balconies, from one of which two young girls peeped out – they were the prettiest girls I had yet seen in Spain: their eyes were like black flames, and with a single smile their mouths said more than any poet can say in a long poem – may Byron and Petrarch forgive me! I reached a big square with an enclosed garden : there were beautiful flowers, palms, rubber trees and all the loveliest tropical plants. The sun was also tropical. There were plenty of *tartanas* around, but in them one sits under cover and sees nothing. I therefore preferred to walk, and in the burning sun I went through the gate and over the bridge as far as the *Alameda*, Valencia's promenade, which runs between the dried-up bed of the Guadalaviar and a whole lot of orange groves, where plane trees and palms cast their shade over whitewashed cottages. There were roads and paths enough but very few people. The sun was so strong that one was tempted to hollow out a cap from a fresh, cool pumpkin and wear it on one's head instead of a hat. In the end I threw myself into a *tartana* and stretched out on the upholstered cushions under its canvas roof, I jogged back to my airy room in the *Fonda del Cid*.

At that moment the diligence arrived from Barcelona – the one we should have taken. It was smelly, dusty and only a ghost of the coach we had seen two days ago. The horses were dripping with sweat, the vehicle itself was macadamized with dust and the passengers limped out like hospital patients. Some were in slippers because during the long journey their feet had swollen in their boots, others were carrying their coats : their hair was matted with dust, which also lined each wrinkled face. This is how the company looked and the wretched centaur, the outrider who had almost grown fast to his horse, was in a worse plight. Four days ago he had mounted his horse here in Valencia from where at a gallop, always at a gallop, he had to proceed, in dust and heat, always in the same position save for brief moments when, at stopping places, he changed horses, and so continued until he reached Barcelona, where he took breath for an hour or two –and so to horse again for the return journey, burnt by the sun, half choked by dust, on his way again, without rest. And now he was here : he stood again on the earth, walked, but his gait was stiff, his face was mummified and his smile that of the sick when one says, 'You look better to day,' and he knows it is not true.

To Valencia belong many of the old Spanish stories about El Cid, who in his own day ranked with the Kings of Spain and still in our days remains the pride of his people. He entered Valencia as a conqueror and lived here in domestic happiness with his noble, heroic wife, Jimena, and their two daughters. As he lay dying, all his dear ones were by his bed : even his war-horse, Babieca, had been summoned there. A moving song says that the horse stood, gentle as a lamb, and looked with sorrowful eyes at its lord, who could no longer speak to it – and to whom it could not speak. Through the streets of Valencia, in the night, went the fantastic calvacade, to *San Pedro de Cardeña*, as the dead leader had decreed. At the head was El Cid's banner of victory, guarded by four hundred knights; then came the corpse. Upright on his war-horse sat the dead man, clad in his armour with helmet and shield, his long white beard flowing over his chest. Valencia's Castile gate was opened, and silently and slowly the procession moved towards the plain where the Moorish army was encamped. Six and thirty Moorish kings lay in the camp : terror seized them when they saw the dead hero on his white horse, and they fled to their ships : many threw themselves into the sea. So runs the story of El Cid in Valencia.

The old city gate, through which the dead man rode in the night of terror and death for the Moors, is still there. I stood in its shade and thought of the hero and his horse – and as I stood there a cheerful boy, singing away, came by on the most wretched nag I have ever seen – all skin and bone, a four-legged symbol of hunger – and my thoughts turned from El Cid's noble war-horse to Don Quixote's Rosinante, both equally immortal in the world of song, the two opposites, Babieca and Rosinante.

Early in the morning of our third day in Valencia, I wandered about the streets without finding anything new or noteworthy. I hoped I would, and therefore had paper and pencil with me, but I found nothing. No – I did find something but could equally well have seen it at home in Copenhagen or in any other large town.

In front of a shop entrance which was as broad as the front of the house, hung a vast article of clothing. It looked like a storm-bell, but made of linen and stretched out taut over hoops of steel or Spanish rushes. It was that garment, known nowadays as a crinoline, in which all women, young and old alike, look the same size : it is as though they are wearing umbrellas round their waists – something which has nothing to do with nature or the good Lord. This vast garment hung there and, since it billowed out over the whole shop front, to it had been pinned all the bits and bobs of haberdashery that were on sale inside – children's socks, scarves, ribbons and fans. The crinoline served as a shop sign, the storm-bell summoning folk to the house – but a bell without a tongue. The Señora must creep into the bell – she is herself the clapper in the crinoline. This sight awoke my imagination and I looked into the future. In a thousand years women will no longer wear crinolines, the name will no longer be used : one will see it only in old writings and when people read these and see pictures of crinolines and how the ladies of our day looked in them, they will cry out, they will laugh and be most amused, 'Dear God – what a funny costume that was !' They will read about its origin, which is in itself a legend, how the Empress, young and fair, in womanly modesty, invented this garment which concealed from the world the fact that she was pregnant – and the dress was becoming. She was clever, she was wise, she was beautiful – and thus all women desired to be. And so they all had crinolines, the fat and the thin, the tall and the short. It looked terrible ! How she must have laughed, that beautiful and clever young woman whose invention had only one purpose.

And so it continued year in and year out, in her land, in the neighbouring lands and over all the world. The bell rang out, 'How pretty it is, how comfortable, how cool !' It was *Anno Crinolino*. . . .

IV

Almansa and Alicante

We were on our way again. It was still dark when the *tartana*
came to take us to the station. The train left at dawn. Not a lamp
shone but the stars were out in all their glory. It was pitch dark
in the narrow crooked streets and there was not a soul to be seen
until we got to the rather squalid railway station, after a very
slow drive. Outside, on the bare ground, lamps and candles were
flickering and there were small coffee stalls where drinking water,
anisette and excellent fruits were sold. The place was busy and
filling up with people and goods. Peasants, swathed in their
burnous-like *mantas*, were smoking cigars, and girls and women
with lots of children hanging on to them sat looking bewildered.

It was long after the scheduled time for departure that the
carriages were unlocked, but once we were inside we were very
comfortable in a first-class compartment : it was roomy with sofa
seats and soft cushions.

Now we were off! It got lighter, the clouds grew pink and the
air was wonderfully clear – it all happened in a flash. We flew
into a land of sunshine, in which tall palm trees held their green
fans high in the luminous air and whitewashed, friendly buildings
lay among fruit-filled orange trees. Vines grew like a woven net
over the earth, with rippling channels of water forming the woof.
It seemed to me that in a bird's-eye view the landscape would
look like an enormous carpet, stitched together with all the colours
that painters have ever put on canvas. We stopped for an uncommonly long time at every station, but at least had the chance
of seeing all the motley-clad people.

With the old Moorish town of Jativa, which with its great
citadel looks very picturesque, the garden of Valencia comes to
an end. From the oasis burgeoning with fruit one comes into the

45

stony desert. The sun beat down and it was as if the stony ground
had stored up heat from yesterday's sun and was now releasing
it into the already too warm air. Farms lay solitary, endlessly far
from each other, their fortress-like walls a protection against wild
beasts and wicked men. Not a tree was in sight and the only green
touch was in some big cacti whose spongy leaves swelled up like
fungi in rock crevices or behind fallen walls. Heavily laden
wagons drawn by six or eight mules gave some life to the otherwise dead, burnt desert. It was as though a devouring flood had
covered the whole landscape, as though the burning air had con-
sumed every blade of grass and left not even the ash thereof
behind.

Suddenly we stopped just outside a big station where the line
branched out into a double track : the one went to Madrid, express with no intermediate stops, the other line was to Alicante,
the object of our day's travel. It was now ten o'clock in the morning and the train from Madrid that we were to take was not due
until six o'clock in the evening. But we could eat or sleep or look
around – perhaps do all three – and the time would go fast
enough. At the station there was a very good restaurant run by a
Frenchman and close by, for the convenience of travellers, there
was an oriental-looking building with a shady courtyard and high
cool rooms where one could get a breath of air and indeed spend
the night if one wished. As to sightseeing, it was only a short walk
to the village of Almansa, well known from the history of the
wars.

The streets of Almansa are straight, broad and unpaved, the
houses low with whitewashed, sloping walls, a hole for the window and, here and there, a wooden shutter that could be closed,
but there was not a single pane of glass to be seen anywhere in the
long street. Each wide doorway was hidden by a rush mat which,
when lifted aside, revealed a wretched, half-dark room where the
inhabitants sat and worked – they could not sit outside, it was too
hot. Each room led out on to a small green plot, with a shading
vine or at least a flowering bush. The few people I met in the
street had black hair, black eyes and brownish-yellow skin. The
street winds down below a steep rock, on the top of which are

the ruins of a fortified castle. Down below where I stood, in a sun
that burnt like the flames of purgatory, lies the church and a
couple of buildings of thick stone, with arms carved over the
entrance. Noble families once lived there; now the halls are
deserted, the walls crumbling, the broken windows loosely
boarded up. From this desolation and solitude one comes upon a
monument, a pyramid with a lion hewn out of stone. It is a
memorial to the Battle of Almansa, when the town was given the
title of honour – 'Fidelissima'.*

I had now seen what the town had to offer and had to make
my way back through the broad, sun-filled street, up between the
dazzling white houses, which contained the light and heat. It was
like walking through a Hindu pyre, a protracted auto de fé, and
when at last I reached my room with its shuttered windows and
the cool rush mat on the floor, I knew what it must feel like to
come from the hot sands of the Sahara into the shade of an oasis.
I sank down, took a breath and had I been capable of a thought,
it would have been that I was in the land of sunshine, and that
my blood was so thoroughly warmed through that I would be
able to do without a stove throughout the whole long winter home
in the North. What a blessing, what a saving that would be! The
warm kiss of the Spanish sun, with sun-hot air, had filled my
lungs and was in my blood : I could think only, dream only of
sunshine. And so one gets acclimatized. As we left Almansa,
blood-red clouds lit up the sky like a procession of torches.

The train made good speed but it would be almost midnight
before we would get to Alicante. It was dark and only at the
various stations were there any lights. People got in and out of
the train and everywhere there was tumult. I thought with some
alarm about our arrival at Alicante Station – there, unlike Barcelona, we had no one to meet us. How would it go? But our lucky
star was shining : once again we had proof of the kindness of the
Spanish people and of their goodwill towards strangers. There
was a young Spaniard from Seville in our compartment; at one
of the stations on the way he was joined by a friend, a young

* April 25 1707. H.C.A.

officer whose home was in Alicante. He was very lively and
insisted on trying to talk to us – and we to him – in a sort of
linguistic-arabesque of French and Spanish, with a lot of guessing
on both sides. We talked about travel, about the highway police –
how good they were – and about life in Alicante. He wanted to
know who I was and what I did, and when I said that I was a
writer and that one of my first dramatic works had been a play
about the Spaniards in Denmark under Zamora,[1] and he knew
about that expedition and the subsequent flight of the Spaniards,
we were quite like old friends. I told him of my delight in his
beautiful country and all the friendliness and good will we had
met. We got to Alicante station; there was a frightful crowd but
our young friend called three guards who were on sentry duty :
although they were on duty and of course armed, nevertheless one
took the trunk, the other the carpet-bag and the third cleared a
path for us to the *tartana* which the officer himself fetched. The
crowd made way for us, doubtless thinking either that we were
important people or perhaps prisoners being escorted to gaol!
But it was all the same to us – we were safely in the carriage, our
two Spanish friends shook us warmly by the hand, told us what
to pay the cab driver and off we went to the *Fonda del Bossio*,
which was situated in one of the broad main streets near to the
Alameda de la Reina.

Lamplight streamed out from the hotel into the dark street. A
broad staircase led up to airy rooms, furnished with rush mats :
all the windows were open but one was not conscious of the
slightest breeze. Wonderful fruit was brought up to us, firm, juicy,
muscatel grapes and sparkling wine – real Alicante. The sound of
the sea was our music while we dined, the stars of heaven our
illumination. It was a summer night such as I had never before
known and I knew that tomorrow would bring another summer
day with another summer night, and many thereafter in sunny
Spain.

Next morning we had to see Alicante. Whitewashed, flat-
roofed houses with jutting-out balconies are a typical feature. A
few streets are paved : the *Alameda* looks like a piece cut out of
one of the Paris boulevards – a small piece that no one would

miss. The trees do not offer much shade, but all the same, people
sit there in rows on the stone benches and look at the passers-by.
A couple of Swedish sailors came along, talking loudly and freely
– they were speaking in their own language thinking that no one
would understand. An attractive young woman, in silk and with
a lace *mantilla*, went by, tripping along on tiny feet. She fluttered
her pretty fan, fluttered her eyelashes with natural grace. 'Look
at that girl, look at that girl,' said the sailors. 'There's a trim little
craft for you,' said the one. 'And she's signalling!' said the other.

Near to the *Alameda*, out towards the harbour, is a long low
building which is a kind of market for butchers, fishermen and
fruiterers. On the wall hung bleeding hares and rabbits, with
joints of meat in all sizes. In the fishmongers' hall there lay on
counters and in tubs fish and sea-creatures of all colours, shapes
and sizes. There was a constant buzz of voices as buyers and
sellers bargained. From meat and fish one went to the vegetables.
Oranges lay in heaps as do potatoes with us; enormous onions
and grapes hung from wooden pillars and seemed to be growing
out of the dry wood. Outside was the main street of the town,
with stately buildings, among which the Town Hall stood out,
with a turret at each of its four corners. The cathedral is some
steps away, hidden in a small street, reached through a damp arch
and half-dark arcade enclosing some sickly-looking bushes and
trees. Inside the cathedral the vaulting seemed oppressive and far
too little light filtered through the heavy, mouldy air. How often
in Spain when service was about to begin have I felt the urge to
kneel with the congregation before the unseen God. But here I
breathed an air that was not the spirit of God, I wandered in a
twilight that was the work of man.

I hurried out of the church into Our Lord's fresh sunlit air,
saw happy people around me, living, noisy people. Girls, women
and children stood on balconies and in doorways: there was
many a motif here for a painter.

The rays of the sun could not reach down between the tall
houses: the balconies met overhead, neighbour could shake hands
with neighbour across the street. The sun burnt fiercely out on
the open square: it seemed to draw into itself yet more strength

from the white walls of the houses, from the dusty, yellow surface of the street and from the arid rocks round the town. There was not a tree, not a bush to be seen. The air was so dry that one's mouth and throat lost their natural moisture. If one wanted to cross by the sunbaked harbour over to one of the open bathing huts on the beach, one had to summon up all one's strength to make a conscious effort to move and then to walk almost like an automaton under the shade of an umbrella. Only in the sea, in the rolling waves, could sluggish, half-scorched limbs recover their elasticity.

Along the beach, beneath the arid, flame-yellow cliffs, stood big wooden cages in which lions and hyenas were on show. Had they ever got free they would have thought themselves still in their own sunbaked Africa. Along the highway there was a stream of carriages, with ladies and gentlemen in national peasant costumes (but of velvet and silk), playing mandolins, castanets and curious, long-necked, stringed instruments.

It was only the next day that we heard from the Danish Consul that, some miles out of town, there was a folk festival: ladies and gentlemen in pseudo-peasant dress had danced far into the night by torchlight in the open square near the sea. It was a pity that we had not heard of this in time to attend. In the town itself one was not aware of this exodus. It was Sunday evening and the *Alameda* was full of people, military, civil, ladies in black *mantillas* with spangled fans, women and girls with coloured kerchiefs. A military band played well past midnight, groups of children danced in the midst of the throng and all the benches were filled with people gossipping away. It was like a popular dance hall. The gas lamps glittered under the dark trees. Down by the harbour, on the other hand, it was lonely and deserted and there were no lights. I saw the stars, great and clear, and I heard the surf breaking, with the music from the *Alameda* in the background. I thought of home, with memories of Danish summer nights, of dancing in the woods under the beech trees, near to the open strand. It was not homesickness that I felt – no, I was happy, with home in my heart and mind.

V

By Diligence through Elche to Murcia

Alicante is one of the main ports of call for the Spanish coastal
steamers.* It would have been most convenient for us to go by
sea to Málaga and from there overland to Granada, but by so
doing we would have to give up a visit to Murcia, which was
described to us as a most interesting town, where we would see
Moorish remains and gypsies and where are found the most
picturesque costumes in Spain. Furthermore, on the way to
Murcia we would go through the most tropical part of the country and see the famous palm grove of Elche, the biggest of its kind
in Europe. We could not miss all that! Of course the most hair-
raising stories of assault and robbery were told of that road, and
the district from Alicante to Murcia and from there to Cartagena
was as notorious as the mountains of the *Sierra Morena*. But our
Consul and every Spaniard to whom we spoke assured us that we
had nothing to fear : the highway police were excellent and all
the roads safe – one could travel with an open purse in one's hand
and no one would take a farthing!

We wanted too to try a real Spanish diligence. We got seats.
The *tartana* was at the door by two o'clock in the morning and
lumbered away with us in the dead of night to the vast warehouse where the diligence waited. Until departure one could
either pass the time outside in the narrow, gloomy street or go
inside where a single lamp and half a candle lit up but sparingly
the objects nearest to them. Most of the light fell on an old man,
half-dressed, who sat in the office, that is to say, on a large crate,
enveloped in cigar smoke. He was the cashier and took the money
from passengers who had not paid in advance. Two armed men

* The Spanish steamers call at Barcelona, Alicante, Málaga and Algeciras:
the French ships between Marseilles and Algiers touch only Alicante. H.C.A.

lay stretched out on the bare ground and an old woman with a
ragged *manta* over her was lying asleep on some sacks. Crates,
chests, harness and bundles of faggots lay mixed up together in
the big shed. The glow of cigars a long way away in the darkness
showed that there were more people here than one could see in
the feeble light.

It was four o'clock before goods and passengers were stowed
away into the narrow, heavy, jolting box of a vehicle which now
moved off creaking, drawn by ten bell-hung mules. I cannot say
that we went at the pace to which we had hitherto been accus-
tomed in Spain – we moved sedately, step by step, as though the
driver were reluctant to leave Alicante's dusty streets. Here and
there we hit a paving stone which, one might think, had been
laid down for no other purpose than to jolt the carriage and us
into wakefulness. I nearly hit my head on the roof of this rumbling box. We drove through the *Alameda* where the lights were
out, past our hotel which seemed to have gone back to sleep. My
fat Spanish neighbour was already asleep before we were out of
Alicante's dusty main road where, in the twilight, the houses
looked like big whitewashed water tanks in a town where water
was scarce.

As it grew lighter, the landscape took form and outline like a
sketch on grey paper. The road was so broad that ten carriages
could have driven on it side by side : in some places it was stony
and level, in others rutted and broken up. The view was bounded
by dark, bare hills. The whole district looked as if it were laid out
for robbery and attack. There was not a living creature in sight.
Solitary buildings were few and far between, large and straggling,
with brick cisterns to catch the rainwater which was sold by the
glass, tepid and greyish. Mixed with anisette it tasted like medi-
cine – it is always as well to know what one's drink tastes of.

The road got worse and worse, in fact it lived up to the most
dreadful descriptions one has ever read of Spanish highways. It
was just as if we were driving over an endless, dried-up village
pond. The *mayoral* whipped the mules, the *zagal* whistled and
shouted '*thiah* !' and thundered out a rigmarole of words – faster,
faster. The heavy-laden vehicle in which we sat rolled violently to

the right but recovered its balance when the wheels suddenly sank into a hole on the left – it had no time to overturn, it was going too quickly. To the birds of the air it must have looked like a ship in a heavy swell. Often it gave a hop over a hummock, which was very disturbing to one's insides! Now we were driving through broad, stagnant pools, with deep hidden ruts, now over stone-hard slopes which had strayed into the road just to upset us – but we were not upset and we went so fast that it could only have been centrifugal force that kept the carriage upright.

And this road, abandoned alike by the gods and the highway authorities, led to the most lovely place – a paradise, an oasis of beauty, like the enchanted garden of Armida.[1] We were approaching Elche and could see the fruit-filled valley and its outspread grove of palms, the biggest and most beautiful in Europe, the most idyllic in Spain. Enormous palm trees stretched up their layered, scaly trunks, surprisingly thick and yet slender in relation to their height. Dates hung in great heavy bunches from stem after stem beneath the leafy green screens. Pomegranates filled the undergrowth, where the brilliant red fruit shone between the dark leaves; and here and there was a lemon tree, the pale yellow fruit contrasting with the red of the pomegranates. As the Spanish saying goes, 'There is only one Elche in Spain.'

During the whole of that day's journey everything we had seen was reminiscent of pictures of the Holy Land. We had driven over scorched stone steppes, slaked our thirst at tepid cisterns; the rays of the sun had burned as they burn in the valleys of Palestine and in the heat we had enjoyed the shade of the palm trees as King Solomon enjoyed it, the shade that the disciples had known in their wanderings.

The rich country around Valencia may be called a kitchen garden; the Elche district is an oriental park, it is the palm-bouquet of Spain, a bouquet miles in circumference. The town itself has about two thousand houses and was much bigger and of more consequence in Roman times when the sea came up there and Elche had a harbour. We drove some way along the yellow-brown walks, which were draped with creeping plants in rich profusion.

We drank our chocolate in the little *venta* where the diligence halted, and after an hour's rest the mules once again shook their brass ornaments, we were again squeezed into the diligence and were on our way. The next stop was to be Orihuela, whose fertile '*campaña*' has given rise to the Spanish saying, 'Rain or no rain, there's always wheat in Orihuela.'*

The ornate buildings in the town, the grand barracks of the cavalry, the Archbishop's Palace and the cathedral – all these I must have seen, but I do not remember them. But the inn where we dined, that I do remember – it was unforgettable. The house, the rooms, the kitchen, the staff – everything about it was as genuinely old Spanish as anyone could wish. From the street one went through into a courtyard crammed with every kind of ancient conveyance – gigs and *tartanas*, carriages from the time of Don Quixote, that gentle knight of blessed memory. Our diligence paraded itself here like a well-trained elephant in the midst of this menagerie of vehicles. Turkeys, hens, cats and other livestock filled the crooked, crannied path up to the entrance of the house, adorned by a withered vine hung about with rags and fruit and vegetable peelings. The doorway had neither door nor curtain, the rooms were crowded with people sitting at tables, which were laid for refreshment; flies zoomed in swarms overhead like great black veils. There was not a vacant chair or bench and one had to go outside and look for a stone or tub on which to sit under an umbrella in the sunshine. The kitchen was the central point for all the rooms. The chimney corner blazed : there was a tremendous frying and roasting going on. Women, young and old, each one less attractive than the next, were hard at it scraping vegetables, cutting meat, boiling, frying and serving, yet everything went at such a leisurely pace and so sleepily and with an air of indifference that was very disturbing to a hungry stomach ! The hostess, a young blonde woman, inordinately fat but with a pink and white complexion, issued orders in a deep bass voice. She looked as if she had good muscles and could doubtless have forced many a man to his knees.

* '*Llueva o no llueva, trigo a Orihuela.*' H.C.A.

She was the real type for a bandit's wife. It seemed to concern her not at all that a new collection of travellers had arrived, and that the diligence had only a short stop here and that we were all in need of sustenance. Several times she was asked to attend to us but she did not answer; it was as though she saw no one, heard nothing. Her smiles fluttered, her chatter, high-pitched and un-broken was directed solely at a couple of favoured guests who were sitting, already served. When, after having waited over an hour, I took her by the arm and asked at least for a glass of wine, she looked at me amazed, gave a half-gracious nod and said, 'Wait your turn.'

And wait I had to, we all had to wait until the mules were again harnessed, jingling, to the diligence and the *mayoral* was cracking his whip – at which moment, at her signal, a couple of old women waddled forward, laid a cloth on the table and produced one roast after another. Madame stood in the middle of the room, her fleshy flabby arms akimbo, and assumed such a welcoming, willing look that it was really funny – she should have been painted as an inn-sign.

We got back into the coach and out on to a road which was, if possible, even worse than the one we had been on before: in hole after hole, up and down we bumped over clods of earth and hummocks made by rain, sun and traffic. It was no consolation that a few steps away from us a good road was being laid down, straight and smooth for comfortable travel, and would be finished in a few weeks' time.

The Queen of Spain was at that moment in Seville: for the first time she was visiting the southern provinces and was ex-pected in Murcia. The authorities were therefore most anxious that Her Majesty should see how excellent the roads were. She would certainly be able only to praise them – wretched travellers like ourselves knew only too well what these excellent roads had been like earlier.

The bare dark hills receded further and further into the horizon. Aloes with their tree-high flowering stems stood thick as plantains. The fields were overgrown with enormous cacti, covered with their ripe, red-gold fruit, and on the higher ground

Spanish peppers, the bright-red pimento, lay spread out to dry in the sun.

A couple of hundred people were busy working on the new railway. We sat and gasped for air, longing for a drop of water. A great big clay pitcher, which had lain hidden under the shadowing cacti, was brought to us. The water was tepid and ill-tasting. The sun gave us an unceasing bath of fire and I began to think that we were not far from boiling point. *Tartanas* were pulled up by the road-side : their horses were fast asleep, the drivers slept, the passengers inside stretched out on the upholstered cushions, and if anyone at that moment thought about the bible, it must have been about the men in the fiery furnace. Not a bird flew in the scorching, dry air – but all the fire and all the warmth seemed suddenly to be concentrated in two big glowing eyes which looked at me as I stepped into a low, flat-roofed house among the huge dusty clumps of cacti. A girl of about twelve, but fully developed, a real Murillo beauty, sat there. She was but scantily dressed – doubtless because of the over-powering heat. She had a heavy juicy bunch of grapes in hand – 'Wine and passion' could have been the inscription for that bacchanalian picture. We were indeed in a hot country!

There was not a breath of wind : the very dust did not have the strength to lift itself up from the road and down in the bed of the river there was not a drop of water. In this state a river can be, as the Spaniards say, 'bled',* and can appear lifeless. Here, as in Valencia, water is piped from the river into the *campaña* which, by means of this artificial irrigation, is transformed into a fertile garden. Vines, maize, beans and love-apples grow in beds between mulberry bushes and pomegranates. We drove down into the waterless river bed, by the side of tall bamboo rushes. The bridge over which we should have driven towered over us like an ancient triumphal arch.

In front of us, in the middle of this great fruit garden, we saw Murcia. The slender tower of the cathedral stood out high above the other buildings, as if it had risen up to bid us welcome.

* '*Sangrado*'. G.T.

1   Andersen, cigar in hand, in the garden of the Collin house in Copenhagen, 18 March 1862. He had learned to smoke in preparation for his visit to Spain.

2 Andersen and Jonas Collin in Bordeaux, 9 January 1863, on their way home from Spain.

VI

Murcia

We drove through unpaved streets, past the town promenade, *La Glorieta*, and the diligence stopped at a *Casa de Huespedes*, which reminded me of the inn at Orihuela. A young grubby *Pepita*, with fresh white flowers in her greasy black hair, took charge of us and without so much as by-your-leave, tried to show us up to two balcony rooms. Her flame-red skirt, deep yellow kerchief and her white, open-worked collar loudly proclaimed her assurance in her own beauty, dirty though her neck and arms were. Cocks and hens scattered as she crossed the courtyard and when she heard that we had chosen a lodging elsewhere in the town she hoisted herself up on the low unsteady railing outside the donkey stall and snapped her castanets and flashed her eyes at us, until we were out of sight of this firework display.

Our trunks and carpet-bag were almost too much for a thin old man who tied them all together and set off at a gallop, the quicker to be rid of them. We soon reached the cathedral and behind it, on the *Plaza de San Leandro*, was the hotel which had been recommended to us, the *Antigua Casa de Hospedaje de la Cruz*. It was no first class *fonda*, but nevertheless the best place for a foreigner to stay in Murcia. It was very good and incredibly cheap. We had two large rooms with balconies looking on to the square and a side-street. We had letters of introduction to the host, Don Juan de la Cruz, and his wife but were told that they were no longer in the house, which was now managed by relatives, young, friendly and very well-mannered people. They asked if we would prefer French or Spanish cooking. We chose the latter and found ourselves very content. We got, in abundance, roast peacock and quails, wonderful fruit and good wine.

We were staying right on the square, behind the beautiful

cathedral. The sound of the organ and the mass wafted over to us, but outside it was otherwise quiet and deserted. We saw some priests in vestments crossing the square, preceded by two choir boys in red cassocks with big lace collars. The church was naturally the first place that we visited here.

Originally it was a mosque and the whole building must then have been very beautiful. But through the centuries it has undergone a great many alterations and has been subjected to over-ornamentation. The great main entrance has been overloaded with scrolls and bas-reliefs, the whole portal is weighed down with heavy stone figures. Although the tower has had several of its slender horseshoe windows walled up and has suffered additions, it is still predominantly Moorish in style. The bell chamber at the top is reached by way of low, easily-mounted steps. In the free air the chimes ring out over town and country.

What particularly interested me in Murcia were the gypsies whom I understood had settled here, as in Granada, occupying a whole district. I was warned not to venture out there alone – they were said to be very quick with a knife. In all the European countries where gypsies are still to be found they are a rootless, outlaw race – for example in Hungary, in England and up in Norway, where they are known as 'Fantefolk'. Without culture or religion, the Gitanos, an Egyptian horde, wandered about on the face of the earth, like other wild animals allowed to live and hunt for their food. Only Spain seems to be a homeland for them. The following day I was to go to the outskirts of Murcia where they lived but I would not, I was told, find the quarter exclusive to this tribe: during the last years Christian families had also gone to live there and some gypsy-born folk have settled themselves in the town itself. There has even been intermarriage between Gitanos and Spaniards. Progress marches on – at the expense of Romance.

From the quiet church square where we were staying, one comes very soon to a busier quarter. Nearby is the Alameda where the weeping willows droop their leafy branches down into the dry river bed. A great walled bridge leads to another square which we found thronged with people. Peasants in picturesque

clothes sat on their equally dressed-up mules, with wife or sweetheart perched behind. Naked children, two or three years old, ran
about getting sunburnt. One had the peel of an orange round his
neck. Laurels and flowering oleanders grow literally in the gutters
and in these was water, clear water which gave itself to the great
river's dried-up course. We discovered that we were not, as we
had thought, on the way to the gypsy quarter, but find it we
would – and did. If I could sketch I would have brought home a
picture from this place.

By a small thatched house, with a dusty oleander bush in full
bloom, stood a black-haired youth, skin as brown as if he had
been rubbed with walnut juice, sparkling black eyes – all the
typical gypsy features. He was sharpening a big robber-knife,
helped by a little nut-brown girl in a bright yellow skirt. One
sleeve of her blouse was missing, but it was a pretty little arm that
was visible. She was turning the grindstone and put her tongue
out at me as I went by.

The shortest way home was through the long main street, the
Calle del Caballeros. The sun was so burning that one began to
look like a gypsy oneself. Not far from the church was a building
that we took for a café, laid out with the elegance we had seen in
Barcelona. There were airy rooms, stone pillars supported the
roof and a large canvas was stretched out over the garden where,
between flower beds and a fountain, there were benches and small
tables on which lay magazines and newspapers. Collin and I went
in and asked for refreshments. The waiter smiled and said that
we were in a private clubhouse, the town Casino, but added that
we were welcome to stay there, to read the papers and do as we
pleased – we were visitors and that was enough, only he must
inform one of the Directors : permission was given at once with
typical Spanish courtesy – they did not ask our names, only which
country we were from.

It was very shady there, but there was no breeze. The heat
dominated everything. One should really have stayed quiet during these sun-hot days and not always have been on the move,
but we 'had running leather in our shoes', which we should have
put on only in the evening, for a walk to the high lying *Alameda*,

from where there is a view over the river and *campaña*, out to the hills. At sunset, the hills are lit up so that they are aglow, but only for a moment – then the light is quenched and immediately the stars come out as if they had been waiting for a signal. From one house came the sound of castanets, but not as one hears them in the north. There they clink as if someone were rattling wooden bowls together; here they are struck in a way that produces a swelling sound in perfect rhythm : they hold their own as solo instruments. We in the north know nothing of the power and mobility of the castanets. . . .

From a small street a funeral procession came across the square. It was the only one I saw during the whole of my stay in Spain. There were lighted candles with long flames and prayers and psalms were being said and sung. I did not understand the words but thought of the old Spanish psalm of Prudentius[1] which is in our Danish hymn-book. It was the funeral of a young girl. There was a procession of clergy with crosses and banners, choirboys swung censers and the mourners followed, each holding a long, thin, lighted wax candle. High on their shoulders, hooded men bore the open coffin on a silver embroidered pall : a young girl lay there like a beautiful waxen image, over her a mantle of flowers and over us all, God's starry heavens. It was as if she were sleeping, as if with song and blessing she should be brought to her chamber. All the watchers on the balconies and all who met the procession on its way paid homage to the dead, she who in her rest was one step nearer to those who have gone before, than are we who are living. From my balcony I watched the procession until it had passed the church and the last flickers of the candles had disappeared.

The evening was very still, the stars very clear and bright. Suddenly the snap of castanets was heard again. And now there was a jingling and a jangling and a heavy rumbling – it was the diligence, drawn by twelve mules hung about with bells and ornaments. Off they went, the lantern in front of the *mayoral* shining on the hurrying mules. And then it was quiet again in the square and in the streets : the guitar and castanets were silent, there was peace and quiet here on earth and in heaven. The stars

above were large and clear and the air beneath so light and yet so
warm – it was good to be alive and to breathe it in.

How long should we stay in Murcia? The first steamer that
went from Cartagena to Málaga would decide this. We would
wait eight days for it, but not longer – then we would go back
again to Alicante from where is a regular steamer service.

One of our friends in Murcia telegraphed to Cartagena for us
and the telegram in reply said that a steamship to Málaga was
expected : we should therefore, as soon as possible, indeed the
next day, make the six-hour drive to Cartagena.

At ten o'clock in the morning the diligence left from the same
Casa de Huespedes at which we were set down four days earlier.
The grubby *Pepita* was standing there again in her flame-red
skirt and bright yellow kerchief, a fresh flower in her greasy hair.
The diligence in which we should travel appeared to consist of
two wooden booths which had been nailed together. Collin and I
got into the first booth with an old priest. The shutters between
us and the back shop were immediately pulled down so that we
had a constant draught on our necks and six people as ballast.
There was a frightful coquette, an affected servant girl whose
tongue ran on without ceasing like a peppermill; then there was
an elderly woman, fat and lethargic, a lump of sleeping flesh, and
in the farthest corner was a person decked out in the most incredibly patched clothes – it was a matter of conjecture as to
which bits of his coat and trousers belonged to the original
garments. There were three other passengers of whom one was in
the better-dressed category. He had a shirt-frill and a handsome
tie-pin, but his linen was so dirty that if he looked like that every
day then he must have hired dirty clothes from some washerwoman or other. The atmosphere in the carriage was a mixture of
tobacco smoke and the smell of onions. I noticed it as soon as I
put my foot on the wheel to get up into the vehicle and had to
to turn round to get a less mixed mouthful of air. I looked up to
the balcony of a nearby house, where a number of women stood
and waved good-bye to their friends : at the very front there was
a pretty child, a little girl of about two years. I waved to her and
she was so shy that in her innocence she pulled her little frock up

over her head. Do not tell me that the young Spanish girls are not modest!

We rumbled off through a crowd of people, out of the town into a shady avenue with gardens, vineyards and mulberry groves, leaving warm Murcia.

VII

Cartagena

For the first hour we were still in the fertile *campaña*, but then the landscape became stony, dry and burnt-out. A strong, piercing wind blew from the sea; all around the countryside was barren, dull and empty of human life. We stopped at a solitary building by the roadside where tepid rainwater, mixed with pungent bad anisette, was offered for sale. At four o'clock in the afternoon we reached Cartagena and through narrow, dark streets got to the *Fonda Francesca*, the hotel recommended to us. We went through long dark passages, and up narrow steep steps: it looked gloomy and dark. The rooms were high and like prison cells; the windows, all with iron bars, were so high up that one would have had to crawl up on to the table in order to look out – or rather in order to look in to one's neighbour through the open door of his balcony which practically touched the windows opposite. Such a room Collin had, while I got one with a balcony door and a little glass window pane in the thick wall. It was not really very comfortable here, unless one regards it as comfortable to be living immediately as in a family – to live with the neighbours without actually being in their sitting-room. There was the width of the street between but this could easily be overcome – one jump and one would be with the family.

Early the next morning, it was barely four o'clock, there was a knock at my door and a servant told me that the steamship which was going to Málaga had arrived and would sail early in the forenoon. This caught me rather unawares: I was tired from the drive and had not yet seen anything of Cartagena. The man said something about another ship going to Málaga either tomorrow or the day after and when I heard of this possibility, I decided to wait.

The Danish Consul, a Spaniard called Bartolomeo Spotturno, received me with much friendliness and charged his son to look after me and my companion. The young man was the Russian Vice-Consul, had been brought up in Germany and spoke good German. He was attention itself and we could not have wished for a better guide : no one could have shown us around with more intelligence and knowledge.

Through the *Puerta del Mar* we came to the harbour which is very extensive and of an amazing depth : a rocky island shelters it from the wind, the twin forts of *Fuerte de Navidad* and *Castillo de Santa Barbara* shield it against an enemy. A wilder, more burnt-out landscape have I never anywhere seen – not a tree, not a bush, not even a cactus, which flourishes in the sun, was in sight. The cliffs both near and far were a tawny colour like peat ash. In the mountains there are silver mines and in the valleys the Esparto grass grows in such profusion that it has given to the town the name '*Spartaria*'. When in a couple of years' time the railway is completed from Madrid to Cartagena, the harbour here will without doubt be the busiest in Spain. Escorted by a young naval officer, a relation of our Consul, we went over by the boat to the Arsenal and saw there the enormous shipyards and the vast dock – a rocky basin, vertiginous, deep. Galley slaves were working everywhere.[1] For the moment preparations for the forthcoming visit of the Queen seemed to take precedence over everything else. In several workshops they were busy carving and painting shields, and other decorations. An artificial garden was being laid out in front of the Arsenal with earth, plants and bushes transported from the country.

Cartagena is low-lying, with only one of its roads going some way up the rocky coast. The view from there over the bay and the sea is incredibly picturesque. I walked up that way alone, mounting higher and higher. I met a peasant on his mule, with two heavy, full sacks in front of him. One had burst open and out of it was dripping some ochre-red stuff. He tried to mend the sack with some old rags and a couple of needles. It was red Almagra earth he was carrying – he told me that it was dug up at a nearby village and used to mix with snuff. I went on a bit further and came to a little windowless house. The only light inside came through the open door. Outside sat a young, pretty girl, mending her bright red skirt. It was a big tear and so she had taken the skirt off and was holding it in her lap. Close by her was a small boy in a tattered shirt. He was leaning against the doorpost, snapping his castanets – but it was not the right sound. I went past but had to come the same way back. Big drops of rain fell and there was a heavy shower, so I sought refuge in the windowless house with the boy with the castanets and the young beauty. She talked with me as if I belonged to Cartagena, as if we saw each other frequently : her whole manner was so womanly, so charming, she could have been of noble birth.

She tossed her head as if she owned all Cartagena and was clothed in silk and gold instead of an old red skirt. She showed the little boy how to use the castanets, with such seriousness that it was amusing. The rain stopped all too soon – and only the rain gave me an excuse to stay there – but I heard her castanets for a long time and when I got down to where the road begins there was, as it were, an answering sound from other castanets being played; when I reached my room I heard them in the house opposite.

There were pretty daughters in that house and some young soldiers were paying a visit : they had thrown off their jackets, the castanets flung out rhythm and melody, snapping out embellishments and trills with true artistry. They began to dance, they laughed, they sang, and someone strummed on a guitar. The sun-warm day turned into a star-clear evening.

There are no sailings from Spanish harbours on Sundays. On the Saturday evening, therefore, we realized that we should have to stay in Cartagena at least for another whole day. Collin decided to make use of the time visiting the silver mines. He is much better than I am in walking long distances and on difficult roads and was therefore able on foot to see much more than I could of the districts surrounding the towns where we stayed. From the hills of Barcelona, Valencia and Murcia he brought home many specimens for his scientific collections and had many a tale to tell about the Spanish peasant. I spent most of the day reading the newspapers in the *Circulo Cartagenero*, the town Club to which we had been introduced by young Spotturno. The beautiful rooms surrounded a pillared courtyard paved with marble – a real grand salon with the sky for its ceiling. Under this ceiling today hung heavy rainclouds, which soon emptied their riches so that the marble floor was flooded and, in an effort to prevent the water from flooding into the open rooms, bags of sawdust were laid down between the pillars.

For the rest, the rain plays no small part in Cartagena. On one of the high table-lands above the town the rainwater collects into a whole lake and if this overflows then it floods down into and over Cartagena. Another unwelcome guest here is the so-called *Mistral*, a cold, harsh wind, whose acquaintance we were also to make. A violent squall arose at the same time as it was announced that the steamship *Non Plus Ultra*, would arrive after midnight and pick up passengers for Málaga.

We were to go with it and a storm was blowing that might subside by morning but could equally well rage for a couple of days : it was an enjoyable prospect. The wind whistled over Cartagena and through the narrow streets. It sounded as if the air were filled with wailing and lamentation. The sea would surely be in a violent uproar. I was in a fever at the thought of it. The storm increased but out there we should and would go ! . . .

It was our last night in Cartagena, Hasdrubal's city, and I dreamt that I was walking on the bottom of the sea. Curious plants, as profuse and strong as Elche's palm trees, waved around and over me. I saw precious pearls – but none had the sparkle of the eyes I had seen in this land of Spain; above rolled the sea with the deep tone of an organ, the music as of a hymn. I was a prisoner in the depths of the sea and longed for life up above in the light of the sun.

When I woke up in the early morning the weather was beautiful; the storm had blown over, every cloud was gone, not a breeze stirred. The harbour was mirror-clear and the ocean, so far as the eye could see, was dead calm. We went on board the steamer and for several hours enjoyed the view of Cartagena and its bare volcanic hills. It was nearly two o'clock before we made for the open sea.

According to all the descriptions we had had, it was a typically dirty Spanish ship on which we had embarked. The deck was crowded with passengers from the second class: there were grubby children, probably all belonging to the same family, who tumbled about, uncontrolled, all over the deck. The parents spread out bedding for their rest and comfort. Collin and I were the only first-class passengers. Our cabin was low, narrow and with extremely dirty sofa cushions. Before I could lie down to sleep, I had to take a piece of clean linen from my trunk and put it round the pillow, which was too greasy to touch without a cover. The mate and, I think, the engineer took their places at the dinner table just as they were, straight from their work, but they were good-natured, unassuming men and the mate knew not only Hamburg but also Copenhagen – he had been that far north. Up on deck, the sun burnt and we had no awning. The sea was calm and became even more smooth and still, quite the reverse of what I had pictured to myself during the stormy night in Cartagena. The sea slept and my fear of it slept too, but it was awakened when I lay in my cabin and it was dark – the lamp had gone out since no one had attended to it. The screw of the ship was making a frightful noise: there was something in the machinery which thumped all the time as if it was doing its best to make a hole in the hull. Every moment it felt as if we were hitting or scraping over rocks. I could not understand it or think out any explanation, so I crawled out in the dark up on to the equally dark deck where not a soul was to be seen except the man at the wheel. The deck passengers lay hidden under sacks and woollen rugs. I looked over the railing down into the deep water. Wonderful great fish glowed as they moved.

I went down again in the gloom and dark and on the stairs met the Captain, a courteous and pleasant man. He had the lamp lit again but I could not sleep. The screw and the pumps – or whatever it was – went on thumping so that in the end I had convinced myself that we were sailing too near in to land and that we were heading for trouble. I clambered up again. The ship was moving like a ship of the dead with not a living soul in sight.

At last light dawned on the horizon, sky and sea became wine-coloured, dolphins sprang up from the mirroring water and turned somersaults in the fresh air, gambolling about in shoals around the ship as if they were awaiting their 'Arion'.[2] The captain ordered the engines cut to half speed, otherwise we should get to Málaga too early, he said – the health authorities always slept late and before they had been on board we would not be allowed ashore, something one had to get used to in Spanish harbours. We steered round the light-house into the harbour and before us lay Málaga with its white houses, its enormous cathedral and its high-lying *Gibralfaro*, once upon a time a stronghold and fortress of the Moors.

VIII

Málaga

We were impatient to get ashore. The sun was burning hot and the deck, gunwale and benches were thick with coal dust from the ship's funnel – it was not pleasant. All round we saw goods and people both being taken ashore and brought on board. Boats were waiting to row us to land, their crews – oarsmen and ragged boys – waved and shouted, making their boats fast to the ship, but there was no sign of the launch belonging to the health authorities and we just had to wait. The harbour was crowded with merchantmen, among them a lot of Danish ships – I later heard that there were no less than twenty-four. The white cross on the red ground waved a greeting to us from home, a foretaste of how much at home we should feel here in Málaga.

One of the passengers, a factory manager from Almadén took us under his wing when we finally got ashore and escorted us to the *Fonda del Oriente,* a well-appointed hotel where they spoke Spanish, French and German. One of the waiters, a young man from Berlin, was especially attentive: he regarded us as fellow-countrymen.

Our balcony overlooked the *Alameda,* with its green trees, fountain and lots of people strolling up and down. There were bare-footed Bedouins in the white burnous, African Jews in long embroidered caftans, Spanish ladies with becoming black *mantillas,* women with gay, coloured shawls, elegant young gentlemen on foot and horseback, peasants and porters – life and movement everywhere. An awning shaded our balcony and here we sat and watched the crowd down in the *Alameda,* enjoying the view over the harbour and the sea. The waiter brought us English ale – a heavenly drink when for several weeks we had had only warm wine and tepid water with anisette. Here one could feel really

69

comfortable. The sun went down, the evening came to life. I sat with a cigarette, rolled in the Spanish way : the first pull always tastes of tobacco but the second – well one is smoking! One throws the stump away and takes another paper cigarette – or an excellent genuine Havana cigar. The lamps were lit before the daylight was wholly quenched, then the stars came out and the crowd below increased. People strolled under the trees on the smooth earth, the paved road filled with carriages and riders. A band played selections from *Norma*. I had to go down on to the *Alameda* and join the throng, to admire the beautiful women with their dark flashing eyes, who so gracefully fluttered their black, bespangled fans, and showed how true is the old Spanish verse :

Una mujer Malagueña
Tiene en sus ojos un sol
En su sonrisa la aurora
Y un paraíso en su amor.

They were a living illustration of these lines. Everyone looked to be in good humour, as if life showed only its sunny side : one had an impression of happiness and the joy of living. . . .

In the time of the Moors the sea came up over the sands to the strong walls of Málaga. Of these only a fragment now remains out by the *Alameda*. The horseshoe arch which forms the gateway tells us at once when and by what race it was built and that here was one of the entrances to the town. Not far away, in a narrow, winding street, a couple of old Moorish houses still stand, with whitewashed walls, but over the uneven surfaces the plaster has flaked, revealing marble pillars. Inside, in the little courtyard, are other traces of marble grandeur. Much has been plastered over; clumsy additions have been made to the buildings as though someone were determined to spoil the impression of their original beauty. Who lived here in olden days? No one knows. At the moment the place is used as a warehouse and store for ironmongery. In the shop, slender marble columns, highly decorated, still rise proudly under the richly carved wooden ceiling; steep stone stairways and narrow passages link up a mass of rooms, each one bearing the stamp of a long-vanished age. The roof swells up into a cupola, 'a half-orange'[1] they called it, highly gilded with different inlaid woods. It is as though the bygone years but sleep herein – but of what they dream one can only guess : in these gracefully proportioned rooms, with their delicate, light windows, their lofty fantastic ceilings, one wondered about the life that had in times past been lived here. Perhaps skilful hands worked here and created masterpieces which we have seen and admired in some place or another; perhaps the most beautiful eyes in Málaga once sparkled in these rooms, or a poet lived here and to the music of the lute sang those songs which are still heard on the tongue of the people. Perhaps the clash of weapons was the music dearest to him who once called this house his own in the time of the Ommayad Caliphs.[2]

Another building stands close by, richer and more indicative of its owner's rank and position. Although the open arcade which led to the courtyard is walled up, the columns and their arches are still clearly discernible and the lovely, open Moorish casements have been preserved. Admittedly the halls and rooms were crammed with crates and all manner of lumber, but all this cannot conceal the ancient splendour. The beautiful, fretted, gilded ceilings seemed to us only a few years old, the ornamentation of the walls looks clean and fresh. In one of the rooms we saw in the middle of the floor a marble fountain with its iron pipe, now dry, through which in times past the cooling water streamed. Outside, in one of the gardens enclosed by high walls, water still ripples in long conduits of hollowed marble, ferns grow from every crack and crevice and a mighty palm lifts its juicy, leafy screen high over a whole copse of orange trees and rose-bushes. It was all so beautiful and yet everything was in decay and abandoned. Once upon a time this garden had been loved and cared for : how delightful it had then been after the heat of the day, to walk here in the star-clear evening or in the moonlight. Fountains sparkled among the sweet-smelling trees. Many a happy moment had perhaps been spent here – perhaps many a moment too of terror, as when the Christians lay outside the walls and hunger and need were rife within.

During my wandering here I imagined that the warm sunshine was like a magic veil, laid over the old house and garden, that had put everything to sleep: when the veil was lifted, then the spell would be broken, the water would splash in the marble fountain, trees and flowers would bloom again fresher and freer than before, and Moorish men and women would rise from their sleep of death to renewed life and work.

When I came out into the street there was a sound of castanets: in the shade of the house sat a pretty young *Gitana*, selling chestnuts.[3] Peasants were arriving with great baskets full of figs and dates; heavy juicy bunches of grapes lay on top of each other, amid decorative red-brown vine leaves. From the memories of old dead times one came out into the living, moving present. It was pleasant to wander about wherever one's feet took one. There was always something new to look at, each picture of life in the south blended with another.

In one of the squares, surrounded by cafés and shops, there is a beautiful statue of a woman holding a torch in her hand. Every evening the torch is lit – it is as if one saw the enchantress Circe from long ago, turned into stone, now awakening with the kindling flame of life, waiting for the dead to rise – as rise they will in the world of poetry when their poet at last comes: this place will awake as did the Alhambra when Washington Irving went there.[4]

Through narrow, twisting streets one reaches Málaga's mighty cathedral, which stands like a marble-hewn mountain, dominating the whole town. It is especially imposing when seen from the sea. Here one comes out again on to the *Alameda* and if one follows it right up to the river Guadalmedina, one is in that part of Málaga where the most life is to be seen – and that not only up in the square but down in the very river bed, which at this time of year was completely without water and in this dried-up condition now transformed into a market place. Horses and donkeys stood down there, hobbled together, pots and pans were boiling over open fires, counters and tables had been set out. But if there should come a sudden cloudburst, a violent rainstorm in the mountains, then the river bed would fill up at once – the

CARICATURE OF ANDERSEN WITH THE CHESTNUT SELLER. Published in the
Danish university students' paper *Svaermere* in April, 1863.

water streams with such a powerful current towards the sea, tear-
ing and bearing everything with it, that there is no time for flight.
We were told that thus, in the spring, oxen harnessed to a wagon
were drowned and with it carried away, because they could not in
time reach the nearer bank. But for the moment the river bed

looked as if not a drop of rain had fallen in years. It was an incredible sight. . . .

Collin and I drove some miles up along the waterless river bed : one of Málaga's wealthy traders, Herr Delius, to whom I had an introduction, had invited us on this trip. He wanted to take us to his villa with its lovely garden, enclosed by an impenetrable hedge of shoulder-high cacti which grew in incredible profusion, stretching far up the hillside. The garden was laid out in terraces, rich in trees of many varieties. There was blessed shade beneath the orange and banana trees. Great pepper trees, their countless rose-pink berries like innumerable strings of pearls, drooped their branches, like weeping willows, down into clear, pale green pools. There were tall palm trees and rare pines like palms but aristocrats of their genus. There was the scent of lemon trees and from the high flowering geranium hedges. Passion flowers hung here as thick as honeysuckle on a country hedge at home in the north. Here in the sunshine wonderful lily-shaped flowers were on display – I thought I recognized them from the arabesque scrolls of silver and gold that I had seen in old manuscripts. But, I was told, the most precious plant here was the green grass. Two great lawns were laid out, so fresh and so well kept that it looked as if every blade had been washed and polished. There was a fresh breeze, almost too cool for us who had come from the deep hot valley and had now walked up to the top of the garden on to the highest terrace. Málaga lay before us, its mighty cathedral looking like an ark on a petrified, foam-white sea.

On the way home, we visited another villa, which had been abandoned by its owner. He had ruined himself by speculating in water, that is to say he had used his entire fortune in building in his garden enormous stone tanks in order to collect all the rain-water from the mountains and pipe it down for use. The garden was a wilderness, the water green and stagnant in the deep cisterns. Collin caught a tarantula, a disgusting eight-legged spider. Creeping things flourished here, but no bird sang. The sun burnt fiercely and was even hotter as we drove down in the dry, stony river bed. We were almost dying of thirst and we were grateful to be given a most refreshing drink from a cactus fruit,

Chumbos,* as it is called, the flower and fruit of which are in the national colours of Spain.

In none of the towns and cities of Spain did I feel as happy and as comfortably at home as in Málaga. The customs of the people, nature, the open sea – each so rich and so indispensable for me – I found here, and in addition, I found what for me is even more important, sympathetic, kind-hearted people. Our Ministry for Foreign Affairs had furnished me with an open letter to all Danish Consuls, in terms so commendatory and flattering that I ventured to expect a good reception, but nowhere was it more sincere than in Málaga, by the young Spanish Consul, Scholtz. It did one good to visit his cheerful, happy home. His wife, Swedish by birth and a friend of Jenny Lind, was so full of vitality and so good-natured. It was as though, in her, something of northern domesticity had been transplanted to the Mediterranean coast. The children, laughing and happy, at once attached themselves to me. The eldest daughter, Trinidad, a girl of about four and a half years but very advanced for her age, said straight out at dinner how much she liked me. '*Papa, a mi me gusta mucho Andersen yo lo quiero mucho!*'

With the Scholtz family and that of the banker, Priesz, as well as with my attentive friend, Herr Delius, I was made to feel so much part of them that I almost forgot that I was in a foreign country. In the *Fonda del Oriente* I met a number of Germans, bachelors living here in Málaga, kindly people whom it was a pleasure to be with. Not a word of politics was uttered – one was spared all that friction. Our conversation was usually about the things of special interest in town, the Moorish remains, literature, bullfighting and the opera. Some of the Danish ships which had been here when we arrived were still in harbour and some of the captains called on me. Not only my fellow-countrymen and those others who were connected with my Danish homeland, but every Spaniard whom I got to know – all were helpful and good natured : holiday-humour was everywhere. . . .

At home in our northern lands, tales are told about dark deep

* Prickly pear – Indian Fig (*Opuntia Ficus – Indica*). G.T.

lakes which lure men to them and where, in the end, drawn on by some unseen power, the melancholy throw themselves into the enticing deep. Something of this extraordinary power of attraction Málaga's Protestant Cemetery[5] had for me. I could well understand that a splenetic Englishman took his own life in order that he might be buried in this place. However, at the moment I am not splenetic and I have a great desire to see more and more of this blessed fair earth. I did not commit suicide but I walked in a paradise, in a most lovely garden. Here were myrtle hedges with blooms for thousands of bridal wreaths; tall geranium bushes encircled memorial tablets with inscriptions in Danish – or perhaps one should say Norse since they were memorials to Scandinavians – and one could also read English, German and Dutch. Passion flowers twined their tendrils over many a gravestone and pepper trees drooped their weeping branches over many a resting place. Here stood a solitary palm, there a rubber tree and in the middle of all the green was a friendly little house, painted in Pompeian style, where one could get refreshments. Pretty children with lively, laughing eyes were playing there. The whole garden is encircled by a hedge of wild cactus, over which one looks down to the broad, rolling sea. I fancied that in the rays of the setting sun I could descry the coast of Africa.

Below the churchyard, the road winds away among the hills. All round grow cacti and aloes; it is all wonderfully wild, desolate and deserted. The road goes by a monastery which Isabella, the Catholic Queen, once visited and to which she presented a carved holy image : priests and people can tell of its miracles. It was as if night dwelt therein, from no window did any light shine out into the evening twilight : abandoned by all living beings, the great building lay there in thought-provoking solitude. It was something of a surprise, turning suddenly into the Granada road, to see living Málaga straight before us, lit with thousands of gas lamps, silhouetted against the blue-green, transparent evening sky.

In convents, in towns and in individual private houses on the route where the Queen was expected, there was much busy-ness. Ever since our arrival in Málaga we had seen great preparations going on for the festivities. The cathedral was already decorated outside with many thousands of lamps. Although it was still some weeks before Her Majesty's visit, the lamps were already filled with oil – but there was no fear of rain. In five months not a drop had fallen, and the sky would continue to be clear and cloudless for a long time yet. On the *Alameda* they were making small artificial fountains, with the water-pipes hanging in the tree-tops. Triumphal arches were being erected and by the landing-stage at the harbour there was already an airy, gently swaying Moorish Hall, made of laths and linen, brightly painted. The walls, balustrades and towers, all of canvas and pasteboard, some already in place, others lying about, looked like theatre decorations in the clear sunshine.

The Málaga authorities were to meet the Queen some distance outside the town – in fact at the beautiful country estate that belonged to the parents of my friend, Herr Delius. He took me to this fine property which, with its beautiful flower garden, borders the main highway from Almeria. There was a lovely view out towards the mountains, over rich vineyards and to the open sea. Taste and wealth were displayed in both house and garden.

Old Herr Delius is a botanist and in his delightful grounds had only tropical plants – a wealth and profusion of plants of which, home in the north, I have only seen specimens and that only in hot-houses. One of the daughters brought me a bouquet, very colourful in glowing red and gold, the colours of Spain. Outside the garden, on the sloping banks, warmed through by the sun but where the night dew never falls, muscatel grapes were set out to dry to raisins. They were covered at night with great rush mats. They were already fermenting and for the time being unsafe to eat. After sunset a cold piercing wind blew in from the sea, a wind such as I had never before experienced in Spain. We hastened off in the light carriage. The lighthouse blazed, the air was luminous; every evening here was festive – and a festival would be awaiting us in Granada, for we expected to be there when the Queen arrived.

We had already written about this to our fellow-countryman, Herr Visby, a son of the pastor in Store Hedinge. He had advised against our coming at this moment, since prices in Granada had

all become exorbitant on account of the Queen's visit. I was sure
that the same thing would happen in Málaga when Her Majesty
arrived. The *Alhambra* was one of the main objects of our whole
journey and we really could not give that up; furthermore the
festivities in connection with the Queen's visit would make our
stay all the more interesting. Consul Scholtz therefore telegraphed
that we would be coming.

The diligence from Málaga to Madrid goes via Granada and
is one of the most expensive journeys in Europe, but one must
consider what this service must cost the owner. The coach is
drawn by from ten to twelve mules which are replaced by another
team every fifteen miles or so. They go at a tremendous pace, not
like our slow stage coaches. Collin and I had to book five days in
advance in order to be sure of seats, such was the present rush of
people to Granada. Departure time was seven o'clock in the
evening, but on the day we were due to travel it had been delayed
for an hour because of a big bullfight here in Málaga. This was
one of the bloodiest I saw in Spain and it made a shattering,
unforgettable impression on me.

It seemed as if the whole town was streaming to the *Plaza de
Toros* when we made our way there in the afternoon. Ladies in
their black silk gowns and *mantillas* tripped on their dainty little
feet through the streets, which were too narrow to take carriages.
Women and girls with motley-coloured silk shawls hurried along;
peasants dressed in their best – velvet jacket and breeches, fancy,
hand-stitched leather gaiters on leg and broad brimmed hat on
head – came swaggering along, cigar in mouth : they carried
themselves as if they were young gentlemen of quality on their
way to a costume ball. Outside the bullring were cavalry with
drawn swords : their horses were restive, they snorted and reared.
Lemonade and fruit sellers, and ragged beggars added to the
throng. The sun blazed down on the white walls.

At last we were inside the amphitheatre and fortunately got
seats in the shade. The thousands who were sitting in the sun
fought against it with fans and parasols. The arrangements and
procedure for this bullfight were the same as we had seen in
Barcelona, but here we saw it in all its brutality and horror. . . .

a score of horses and five bulls had been killed and there were still seven bulls left to fight, when I decided that I had had enough. I was so nauseated that I left the arena, after which the fight became even more bloody and – as I was told – more interesting : it continued until all twelve bulls had been killed.

It is a brutal, horrible form of popular entertainment! I heard many Spaniards express the same opinion : they said that it would not go on for much longer and that recently a petition for the discontinuance of these fights had been presented to the *Cortes*.

When we arrived to take our places in the diligence, Consul Scholtz, his wife and little daughter Trinidad were there to see us off, and at the last minute Herr Delius brought me letters of introduction to friends in Granada. It was seven-thirty before we left. Ten mules, their harness bells jingling, took off in a gallop through the *Alameda*, down into the dried-up river bed, past the low, whitewashed houses, from which lights twinkled through the open doors.

IX

Granada

The route that the diligence now takes over the mountains from
Málaga to Granada is longer than that previously taken over
Vélez-Málaga and Alhama by travellers on horseback. That way
used to be very unsafe and for this reason people travelled in
armed convoy. It was common practice for individual travellers
to make a bargain with smugglers who were in control of this
route and knew the district and conditions.

It was dark when we reached the mountains: the powerful
light from the carriage lantern showed us bare rocks and deep
ravines – deeper than we could see, since the light could not reach
below the level of the road. At this point we were joined by
armed soldiers on security guard, whose duty it was to escort the
diligence on this most desolate part of the journey. It was less
than a year since an ambush had taken place, the only one indeed
that people could recall in recent times. The robbers had been
caught the next day! They were peasants, a family whose
youngest son had to do military service, and in order to get money
to buy him out they had taken to robbery.

The carriage light shone out into the wide, barren countryside.
There was a wind and the air was heavy and grey. Collin and I
had corner seats; a good-looking young Spaniard sat between us
and slept the long night through. I could not sleep and longed for
daybreak so that I could look around me. It first grew light when
we approached the little town of Loja which is set very pic-
turesquely on the top of a rock. The river Genil forms a waterfall
in a cleft in the mountains, *Infiernos de Loja*. The outstanding
feature of the town is its cool, fresh spring-water. For us, who for
several weeks had had only tepid drinking water, this was truly
refreshing. Through rich cornfields and vineyards we soon

reached Santafé. In the war against the Moors, the army of
Ferdinand and Isabella set up a great camp here : it was burnt
out in one night, but since the royal couple had sworn to stay
there until the Moors were expelled, work began at once on a
new town with walls and towers. It was here that Columbus was
for the first time received in audience. The remains of the walls
of Santafé fell in an earthquake in 1807. The open countryside
now lay before us, rich and fertile. Olive woods and vineyards
flourish on earth once impregnated with the blood of Moors and
Christians.

At last we reached the outskirts of Granada and from there
into the city seemed an endless way. We drove through long
streets, following the old walls until finally we stopped at the city
gate, but there was so much traffic and so many people that it was
not easy to slip through. Laden mules wanted to get in, ox-drawn
wagons wanted to get out, but in the end we drew up on the
Alameda at the office of the diligence company, where our fellow
countryman, Herr Visby, met us and escorted us to a good hotel
nearby. We were given two good, light rooms looking out on to
the promenade with the snowcapped heights of the *Sierra Nevada*
in the background. Under our windows it was swarming with
traffic and people : the church bells were ringing, we could hear
music and singing. It seemed a very pleasant place to be in ! Herr
Visby pointed out to me, on the top of a hill near the town, an
old wall with a reddish, square tower. There did not seem to be
anything very noteworthy about it – but this was the *Alhambra*,
the famed, enchanting *Alhambra*, the object of our whole journey.
A villa up there caught the eye very much more and with its
white walls looked more promising. It belonged to a wealthy
private individual. We wanted to see everything, but today would
concentrate on the quarter where we were living.

The whole city was busy and in a state of turmoil; the Queen
would arrive in three days with her Consort, children and a vast
entourage. It was the first time since Isabella the Catholic that
Granada would see its Queen.

In front of the main street, by the *Alameda*, had been raised a
triumphal arch of wood and paper, painted to look like marble,

with statues of plaster and linen. When lit up in the calm evening and night the whole thing might be very impressive, but now in the sunshine it looked rather like theatrical scenery. Everywhere in the streets, where old buildings were being pulled down, all signs of demolition had been covered up and hidden under great set-pieces of paper and linen, painted to look like hewn blocks of stone. In places where there had once been monuments, obelisks of lath and linen had been built up on the old foundations. I thought of the Empress Catherine's travels in Russia, where whole towns of scenery and folding screens were put up so that, at a distance, Her Imperial Majesty could be pleased to see how thickly populated the broad countryside was.

Near to the river Darro, in the bed of which gold is found, but which in its present dried-up state resembled only a gutter, there lay an old Moorish-style building. Through its horseshoe gateway one came into a great courtyard overgrown with grass : a heavy jet of water splashed in the stone pool in the centre of the court and this was itself overshadowed by a single massive vine which spread its thick branches over the whole, very considerable, space. Two donkeys and a dozen or so mules stood inside the courtyard, which was strewn with old saddles and harness. It would have been a perfect setting for the dubbing of Don Quixote as a knight, in the inn which he took for a castle. A young girl in flame-red skirt and white blouse – Lindaraja[1] could not have looked better – sat on the edge of the pool and washed her face and neck. . . . One attractive picture superseded another, there was so much new to see. Even in the smallest houses, the entrances were worth looking at : the floors everywhere were paved with mosaic, a kaleidoscope of different figures, vases, flowers or a spread-eagle. But what I most wanted to see was the *Alhambra*. The next morning Collin and I went up there.

From the dried-up bed of the river Darro the road ascends to the city walls. An old gate, with the arms of Charles V carved in stone, leads out into an avenue thickly lined with poplar trees : it is the same road along which the Moorish kings rode with banners waving and trumpets sounding. Now they were busy hanging up coloured paper lanterns, to bring oriental splendour into the long, dark avenue when the Queen visited the *Alhambra.*

From the avenue there is a shorter but steeper path up to the left. Water welled up, splashed and rippled in the verdant undergrowth; slender cypresses and tall poplars stretched up into the blue sky in front of the *Alhambra*'s ancient red walls. By a great, carved, marble fountain the path turns and one is in a long avenue of poplars,* close by the *Puerta de la Justicia,* over whose horseshoe arch is carved an open hand with outstretched fingers; on the opposite side within there is a key. The master builder's words in connection with these two symbols are well known : '*Alhambra*'s walls shall stand until the hand shall grasp the key.'

Two soldiers guard the gate : through it one climbs up between the old walls on to a broad terrace, from every side of which there is a wonderful view over the city and *campaña.* If we stand up here between the two deep wells and turn our backs on the ruins of walls and towers which enclose the vineyards and kitchen gardens, then in front of us we have the whole of the *Alhambra* hill. The Moors dug these wells : clear ice-cold water was raised up from the depths of the earth and used to be carried in great clay jars into Granada by mules. A couple of women sat by the walls and sold water by the glass. We met many foreigners up here. A great many workmen were bowed down under vast bundles of flowering myrtle, coloured lamps and painted paper shields for decoration, which looked out of place and cheap in these mighty, majestic ruins. The whole domain, rich in memories is like a vast Acropolis. Nearest to us, and dominating the whole, stands Charles V's unfinished castle, a four-cornered building of mighty stone blocks. It was his will that in splendour and size this should surpass everything the Moors had built up here and in order to make more space part of the *Alhambra* was torn down : but the royal work remains unfinished – beautiful indeed, but a colossus without a roof, with windowless casements through which the wind whistles. In honour of the Queen's visit these walls too had been hung with countless coloured lamps.

Behind the castle lies the church of *Santa Maria de la Alhambra*

---

* *Alamo* is the Spanish for poplar tree : hence *Alameda,* Poplar-walk, where one walks beneath poplar trees. H.C.A.

and behind that is a little cluster of poor houses and great vine-yards. Under the knotted vines are often found the remains of rich mosaic pavements, of fallen Moorish cornices and arches, all beautifully carved. After a stroll there, one returns to the great terrace and from the rocky height looks down over cypresses and poplars to the deep-flowing Darro. But, one asks oneself, where is the real *Alhambra* with its Lion Court, the hall of the Ambassadors and Lindaraja's enchanted garden?

From the terrace by Charles V's unfinished castle one can see, by the wall, a couple of small, sunken gardens with a few low houses; behind these, in the fastnesses of the walls, within the ruined towers, there under an unostentatious shell, must the enchantment be sought.

From one of these small houses, through an ordinary little door, one enters the rich courts and halls of the Moorish kings. I had great difficulty in obtaining permission to go in: they were so busy with the decorations in honour of Her Majesty the Queen. But a couple of friendly words and a few *pesetas* secured admittance.

It was beautiful but surprisingly small. I did not find it as large and extensive as I had expected. All the same, as I wandered through these arches, these courts, these halls, they seemed to grow bigger. I felt as if I were in a fantastic, petrified lace-bazaar, where fountains played, clear and sparkling, where waters rippled in channels cut in the marble floor, and filled the great pools where goldfish swam. The lower part of the walls is covered with porcelain tiles : the walls themselves are of unpolished white-gold porcelain, resembling marble, but so skilfully carved that it looks like a lace veil laid over a red, green and gold background. Scrolls and inscriptions are interlaced in arabesques, in and out of each other : at first sight they seem rather confused, but when one looks at them properly one can see a regular pattern. On some of the scrolls are inscribed verses in praise of God and his prophet Mahomet, and the walls bear witness to the great achievements of the Moorish kings, to knightly valour and the power of beauty. The *Alhambra* is like an old, illuminated manuscript, full of fantastic, entwined picture-writing in gold and other colours :

each room, each court is another, different page – the same story, the same language and yet always a new chapter.

The *Sala de los Embajadores*, where the Moorish kings received foreign ambassadors, still retains the greater part of its ancient splendour. But how does one describe this in words? What help is it to say that the walls from top to bottom appear to be covered with a veil, over gold brocade and purple, and that this veil is in fact carved stone, filigree work into which light is admitted through horseshoe window arches, set on light marble columns. Over the casements, carved, open rosettes give more light so that one can see the carved wood roof in all its beauty. A photograph, not words, could reproduce such a picture, but even so, it would concentrate on a single spot – one must move around in order to understand and enjoy this beauty in its entirety – go to the open window, look down into the narrow, wild, romantic valley through which the Darro flows, and then turn round and look through the open hall towards the airy light arches, on which the decoration looks like petrified climbing plants, surrounding arabesque scrolls.

The Court of the Lions is equally splendid. Brussels lace, woven in porcelain, tulle-embroidery worked in stone, supported by slender marble columns, here form partition walls, arches, pavilions and alcoves. The lions, on the other hand, are poorly sculpted: clumsy and heavy, they lie around the fountain in the centre of the court.

To the left, out towards the Darro, one goes into the Hall of the Two Sisters, so called after two enormous slabs of marble in the floor. Workmen were busy decorating – as they were pleased to call it – the great hall which was in itself of great beauty. Heavy carpets of damask and velvet edged with gold lace and tassels were being hung over the walls: they covered up too much of the real splendour, leaving only the roof free to be seen and wondered at in its undisturbed, uncluttered, ancient glory. It was there on high, with its gold and carving, and one looked up into it as into the cup of a wonderful and beautifully formed flower.

On the other side of the Lion Court, one goes straight into the Hall of the Abencerrages. It had so far escaped 'decoration' and stood in its original tasteful beauty, from Moorish times. In the centre of the hall we saw the enormous marble bowl, still stained with the innocent blood of the Abencerrages: it has soaked into the stone and has from generation to generation indicted the unfortunate Boabdil. This is, we were told, the only haunted room. Here there is groaning in the night and here strange cries are heard and the wailing of unhappy spirits.

We were taken through a whole labyrinth of galleries, pavilions and rooms, and then stepped down into a small courtyard and into charming bath chambers, at the entrance of which stood marble nymphs and grinning satyrs. Light, rather muted, fell through star-shaped apertures; great marble baths invited use. In the walls the iron pipes which carried the hot and cold water can still be seen. Ascending a few steps again, one goes through a series of galleries, with arches supported by slender marble pillars, and looks down into small flower gardens and into courts with statuary, from there reaching a kind of pavilion, *El Mirador de Linda-raja*, which could not be more lovely, elegant or tasteful. *El Mirador* is an oriel suspended, as it were, over the green-clad cleft in the hills, over poplars and cypresses, and from it one has a view over the city and the nearby vineyards and mountains. Our visit was only short because here too there was decorating to be done. The whole place was in a turmoil. It was, I think, permissible to arrange flowers in pots in the Myrtle Court in order to give more foliage and greenery between the great marble basins but they were even using paper palms – and this in a land where the palm tree grows. For me it was as though I saw a beautiful old statue decked out in carnival streamers.

'An architectural dream' is how Hackländer[2] has described the *Alhambra*: the dream had become a reality for me and one I shall never forget. I returned to Granada overwhelmed by what I had seen.

From Herr Schierbeck in Barcelona I had a letter of introduction to his Spanish brother-in-law, Don José Larramendi; on the letter was his name and title, *Teniente Coronel de Regimiento Córdoba*. When I enquired after him I received yet further proof of Spanish courtesy and readiness to assist a stranger. In the

Fonda de la Alameda, where we were staying, several high-ranking officer were billeted among them a General. Outside his
door a soldier always sat and I asked him about the Córdoba
Regiment. The man immediately went out with me into the street
and led me around and about, all the time making enquiries, but
in vain. In the end he took me to a military office where we were
given Colonel Larramendi's precise address, to which he then
escorted me. I wanted to pay him for his trouble, but he looked
at me with big, wondering eyes, shook his head and would not let
himself be persuaded into accepting payment for his services. He
accepted my hand and thereafter my daily greeting when I passed
him in the corridor.

Through a little courtyard with a fountain splashing among the
laurel hedges and pomegranate bushes, I came into rooms where
Larramendi, his wife and mother-in-law lived surrounded by a
flock of children. I was received as if I were a long-expected, dear
friend. Few people have shown such indefatigable zeal in being
of assistance to Collin and myself as this dear man throughout
our stay in Granada. Not a day passed without his calling on us,
with some happy suggestion as to how we could best spend the
day, and he often sent his servant to us to carry out any errands
we might have had, which he could perform for us better than
strangers in the hotel. I know that he often worked late into the
night to get his work done and so have more free time to be with
us. He was a good, thoughtful man, young in heart and mind,
and our contact with him made our life in Granada the more
agreeable. He spoke some French, Collin had made great strides
in Spanish, and where my vocabulary failed there was always
invention and mime. Accompanied by Colonel Larramendi we
went to a number of places decorated for the Queen's visit to
which, as foreigners, we should otherwise not have been admitted.

One visit we made with him was to the splendid barracks of the
Córdoba Regiment, which are near to the city, between the rich,
abandoned Cartuja monastery and the gypsy quarter. The broad
square by the city walls was, not so long ago, hazardous to visit
in the evening – and even more so at night when assault and
murder often took place. Now here, as in Granada itself, there

was security and at the moment it was all festively decorated with flags. A handsome tent had been put up in the Spanish colours of red and gold : it was in three sections, the floors laid with red velvet. It was here that the Queen was to be greeted by the city authorities on her arrival.

The square was crowded with townsfolk, peasants, soldiers and gypsies. It was noisy and lively. Mules snorted, dogs barked; a street singer raised his snuffling voice, a blind man improvised verses and his boy sold printed ballads. I gave the blind man a *real*; Larramendi told him that I was a foreigner from far away, from the other side of France, and at once he improvised a verse to me which, naturally, I did not understand but the crowd around all applauded him loudly.

The sun was infernally hot and it was refreshing to go into the officers' cool guardroom. Fresh spring-water from the *Alhambra* wells misted the carafes with dew and the long, thin, sugar biscuits, *azucarillos*, disappeared as by sleight of hand when they were stirred into the water in the glasses and gave a pleasant taste. Cigars were passed round and it was all very friendly.

The courtyard was crowded with soldiers. We inspected the dormitory, a large airy room with a beautifully carved ceiling in Moorish style. We saw the store-room with every item of clothing from shirts to handkerchiefs; the kitchen shone with polished pots and pans. In the sick-room the air was fresh and good. We went into the sutler's house : on the floor were heaps of dried cod and piles of round loaves. Enormous onions hung on the wall and over them was a holy water stoup and a large, wooden cross.

I wanted to put some of my impressions down on paper, but I knew I had no paper at home and I therefore went with Colonel Larramendi to a stationer, to whom Collin and I were introduced as visitors from the land of Denmark. We spoke of Zamora's stay there and when I wanted to pay for the paper the answer was, 'It is paid for!' Larramendi had given the sign which Spaniards give in cafés, that the stranger was his guest. I knew that I would not be allowed to clear up the matter, but when, a week later, I went into the same shop to buy paper, I received the same answer

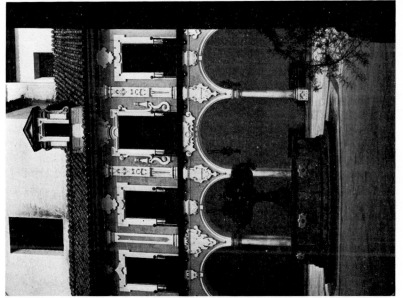

3   Valencia cathedral.

4   A typical patio in Cordoba.

5   The Generalife Gardens, Granada.

when I came to pay. 'It is paid for.' 'No,' I said, 'that is not possible – today I am alone, there is no one with me.' 'Oh no,' said the stationer, 'I am with you, my house is yours.' Naturally, I did not feel that I could go there again, but I must tell this story as an example of Spanish courtesy and attention.

It was on Thursday, 9 October that the Queen was to make her first entry into Granada. From early morning the streets were thronged and what a show it was! Over all the balconies were hung coloured, gold-embroidered draperies, or at least a white cloth decorated with a red border. Flags and banners waved, balloons and garlands of flowers hung so close that they formed a complete sun-canopy over the broad street. In the long lane behind the old Moorish shops, long red and white streamers hung from the top to the bottom storey, fluttering like the veils of the air-spirits in a ballet of the sylphides. Great glass chandeliers, over each a swaying gold crown, had been hung up. Everything looked as though it had been arranged by happy children. The balconies were full of people, mostly ladies – a wealth of Spanish beauty – and what a variety of colour there was in the clothes, especially down in the streets. The peasants from the *campaña* and the hills were so arrayed that they were worth painting. Everywhere were groups, subjects for an artist. There came a farmer on his ass, panniers in front of him, and in each sat a pretty little girl, presumably his children. They had come to Granada today to see the Queen and all this splendour. Their eyes shone with wonder and happiness.

Her Majesty was not due to arrive until four o'clock in the afternoon. We heard that she had reached the reception tent half an hour earlier than the authorities who were to greet her and that she had to wait for them.

There was great rejoicing. All the church bells rang, flocks of gypsies danced through the streets with castanets and strange, stringed instruments – a noisy bacchanalian procession. The black-haired, brown-skinned figures were wonderfully and wildly decked out. I was reminded of children who, when they are playing charades and have permission to use whatever they like from the wardrobe, always take *everything* and wear it all at once. The

D

gypsies had also taken everything that shone and sparkled – silk ribbons, silk kerchiefs, flowers and gold ornaments hung in their hair. They rushed on through the streets, over the squares. From the balconies and garden walls the onlookers applauded, the crowds increased, bands played, trumpets sounded a fanfare, *'Viva la Reina'*.* Roses were plucked petal by petal – the whole rose would be too heavy in its fall – and some petals fluttered down on to the Queen, who sat in a carriage drawn by beautiful white Andalusian horses.

The Queen looked amiable and happy. There was something so open and frank in her face that it evoked confidence and loyalty. The enthusiasm for her seemed to be genuine and great. The King sat by her side and facing them were the young Princess and her little brother Alfonso, Prince of the Asturias. The procession drove to the cathedral, the Queen's first visit. The smoke of the incense poured through the open door which was surrounded by people : they hung on and clung on to walls and statues wherever they could get a foothold.

From the church the Queen drove through the cheering crowd to the house specially and festively prepared for her. Handkerchiefs waved, rose petals fluttered down. The sun-clear day turned into a brilliant evening and Granada was now a fairy-tale city – one was in the magic world of *A Thousand and One Nights*. High over the street, coloured lamps hung like a carpet or like a cloud of sparkling humming-birds.

From here, through a triumphal arch, one came into the new *Alameda*, which runs along the Darro towards the city walls. The houses vied with each other in the invention of different kinds of illumination. Our hotel was but poorly lit, which made the great

---

* Isabella II, born on 10 October 1830, is the daughter of Ferdinand VII and his fourth consort, Maria Christina. Only three years old, she came to the throne under her mother's regency. The late king's brother, Don Carlos, claimed the throne. Bloody civil war broke out. Maria Christina made a morganatic marriage with Don Fernando Muños, an officer in the Life Guards, who was later made Duke of Rianzaras. By this marriage the mother could not, according to the laws of Spain, be the Regent; she withdrew and Espartero took over the guardianship. In 1843 he was overthrown and Isabella II was declared of age. She has married Franz, Duke of Cadiz, who has been given the title of King. H.C.A.

barracks³ in the neighbourhood shine all the more brightly. There were rows of lamps in every corner, in every nook and cranny, which outlined in fire the whole form of this amazing building, in the construction of which the rubbish from every conceivable style of architecture appeared to have been used. There were heavy walls from an old Gothic castle, spiral columns such as are found in King Solomon's temple and in the niches stood rococo statues, grenadiers with bishops' mitres, each piece more singular than the last.

An immense throng of people streamed up and down : all the benches were full and people sat on chairs outside their houses. But further out, where the new *Alameda* ends, was also the end of the illumination and the promenade. It is here that the real old *Alameda* begins and, at an angle, goes along the city walls. I know no promenade as splendid as this, so genuinely southern, so heavenly during the hot summer. Here it was completely deserted, with not a person, not a lamp to be seen.

Ancient, wonderfully tall trees stand in rows, intertwining their thick, leafy branches, and forming on high a green impenetrable roof. At the sides, laurel bushes, oleanders and thick hedges also give protection against the strong sun. The Genil runs close by, soon to unite with the Darro. Clear water runs in stone-hewn conduits on both sides of the avenue, and there are two enormous fountains, decorated with wildly fantastic figures. Only in arabesque scrolls have I seen the like – something between a plant and a human monstrosity. In their enormity these peculiar, baroque, troll-like figures have a strange power : one cannot tear oneself away from them. The fountains stand there, examples of the decoration of a bygone age, but still living with their sparkling streams of water. The faint sunshine which by day filters through is like a smile from those past times. In the evening, the darkness here is as it always was, unchanged. No gas lamp allows the light of the modern world to shine in here. The festive splendour for Isabella II could not penetrate the shade of this sanctuary.

'Now everywhere in Spain is completely safe,' said one. 'Although,' added another and another, 'after sunset in Granada you should not walk alone in the old *Alameda*.' But it was just that place which was so enticing, so removed from everyday life – and now when the new *Alameda* was so chock-a-block with people, when everyone was so happy with all the festivities and so filled with enjoyment, who would stoop to evil? It was so tempting to come away from the noisy throng, so alluring to walk into the almost gloomy darkness of the great, silent avenue, where only the rippling water spoke of life and movement.

I took several steps forward, holding my hand out in front of me so that I should not run up against anything. Far down the avenue I saw a light which moved. Someone was coming with a candle in their hand. The air was so still that one did not need a lantern – one could safely carry a lighted candle, it would not blow out. A young girl came towards me, a child – but here under the Spanish sun she would be called a lovely young bride. She was so frightened at our meeting, poor child : she had not expected to meet anyone here in the dark remote *Alameda.* She was coming from a friend whose mother was accompanying her; they were going to the other side of the illuminated promenade. The girl was her own torch-bearer, she herself carried the candle which shone into her lovely face. She stood still, trembling, like a gazelle about to take flight. 'Do not think ill of me,' she said. 'I think only good,' I said, speaking as best I could, but obviously in such incredibly bad Spanish that quickly that blessed humour, which Cervantes has taught us is native to this land, gave her confidence again. 'You are not Spanish,' she said. I told her that I was from high up in the North, from Denmark where, once upon a time, the Spaniards had been and we had liked them.[4] 'I was a child then,' I said, 'and a Spanish soldier took me in his arms, kissed me and pressed a picture of the Madonna to my lips : it is my earliest memory – I was three years old at the time.' She understood what I said, she smiled and took my hand. Her hand was so soft, its pressure was like a kiss, a child's kiss. . . .

On the squares triumphal arches had been erected, mostly in Moorish style. The most splendid was on the great square near to the Bivarrambla gate where, in olden days, the tournaments were held. Now, as then at those festivals of which so much has been written and sung, all the balconies were brilliant with gay hangings and beautiful women, and where the jousting place itself had been were now planted small gardens, with water springing out from artificial lilies and tulips.

On the *Plaza Nueva* where the street ends above the Darro was a tableau of painted tin figures, representing Moors and Spaniards in battle. They stood on small moss terraces, shooting at each other with jets of water. Myrtle twigs were stuck all round representing great trees. There was always a crowd of children and countryfolk here, enjoying themselves. But one could also, now and then, see something to shock the eye. I saw a cripple, born with only one arm – and in order that this should be seen, the shirt sleeve had been torn off : right up on the shoulder, where the arm should begin, there was a small piece of flesh which looked like a finger. It had only one joint and this moved all the time in order to attract attention. By the entrance to the church lay two albinos, beggars, father and son. They seemed to sleep, always to sleep, while the air shook with the clang of bells and the shouts of welcome. Once, as if sleepwalking, the father raised himself up, blinked his red eyes between the white lashes and stretched out his hand for alms. Here in front of the church people would surely be in a mood for charity. They were two wretched, defenceless bats in human shape. The white mouse and the white rabbit were their light-shy comrades, the day was their torment, the night their time for living – but now the night was as dazzling as the day, a very sea of light shone through the ancient city of the Moors.

Different indeed but not more gorgeous had been the pomp and splendour when the Zegris and the Abencerrages in golden armour with waving banners and scrolls rode out to battle and knightly jousting. The crescent moon glittered and the beautiful daughters of the East looked down from their silk-hung balconies. I had been witness to Granada's most splendid festival of modern times : it burned itself in my memory with all the brilliance of the East and the glory of the sun. . . .

I had not yet seen a Spanish comedy or ballet, it was not the season, but here in Granada, because of the influx of visitors for the royal visit, they had opened the theatre, which was close by the *Fonda de la Alameda*. The interior had been painted up and decorated with red and green silk hangings, but on the stage itself were the most tattered folding screens I have ever seen. That evening a short play and a ballet were to be presented.

In a foreign country where no one knows you or indeed wants to know you, you can, without reservation, be yourself; you are not preoccupied, consciously or subconsciously, with untold doubts – you need not fear that your opinion will be trumpeted forth like the cracking of a whip in the Alps, causing an avalanche of mortification to roll over you. You can see and note the short-comings of those at the top of the bill and dare to enjoy and applaud talent as yet unrecognized.

It was with this comfortable feeling that I arrived at the theatre and with this same feeling I sat and endured the grinding of the wretched orchestra. I resigned myself to the tawdry scenery, resigned myself to the comedy which was so clumsily put on – almost disregarding the audience – that I realized at once that it had nothing at all to do with art. All my expectations were centred on the one high spot – the Ballet. I did not know Spanish ballet and had not seen Spanish dances in any theatre in Spain. Only in the streets of Murcia and Cartagena had I felt the beat of the castanets, struck by ordinary people, and had seen the *Bolero* and *Sequidilla*. Those gracious dances could become pas-sionate – what would the stage have to offer?

The ballet began, it ended, I saw the whole thing. A fearfully tall fellow, who looked like a clumsy journeyman, stepped forth in a cloak and with a guitar: he twanged the strings. His lady-love appeared with a fan at the window and then came down into the street, but they did not have time to dance out their love. Her father came out of the house, the lover threw his cloak over her and she ran away. But now, to give her time to make her escape, he stood himself in front of the old man with a cigar and asked for a light. This request could not of course be refused: they jumped about – it was very difficult to get the cigar going and when it was at last alight the maiden was far away. They dashed after her. *Changement*! The scene changed to a sort of park where a collection of girls were assembled. They danced with castanets, but it sounded and looked as if they had not yet learnt how to do it, indeed as if they had never been in Spain. It was a very select collection of ugly women – it must have been very difficult to find so many in Andalusia. The lovers entered and the girls at once asked them to dance, jumping up and down to show them what was wanted. The dance began, but then the father arrived and he got into good hands : every other girl seized him and twirled him round, every third girl gave him a 'snaps', which he drank and became very merry. The lovers kneeled, he blessed them and the whole company danced the *Madrileña*. That was the ballet.

I clasped my tiny hands and shouted, not 'Allah' but 'Bournonville, Bournonville, how great you are!'[5] I hurried out into the fresh air, into the illuminated city over which the moon was sailing. I would not go again to the theatre in Granada, I had seen Art there.

The next day the Queen drove up to the *Alhambra* and on to Banker Calderon's beautiful villa. From a garden in the street near to the city gate we were to see the whole procession. Colonel Larramendi escorted us there. An elderly Baroness and her daughter lived in the house; there were a lot of visitors, mostly ladies. We sat on the garden walls and terraces, under great trees with pomegranates and quinces. The ladies plucked roses and let the fine petals flutter down over the Queen as she drove past. The young servant girl of the house, in black silk like the others – but the prettiest of them all – also let the rose petals fly. She knew quite well that I admired her beauty and she picked a scented flower, gave it to me and darted away as a swallow flies – and one must let it go thus.

I saw the Queen a couple more times from my own balcony. With her Consort and children she was driving out into the *campaña* to see a laurel tree under which Isabella I hid herself when, during the war against the Moors, she was once nearly captured. The tree and the little estate on which it stands had now been bought by the reigning Queen. The road out to this place crossed the Genil and Darro at the point where the two rivers meet. The water in the bed of the Darro was for the moment no broader than a gutter, one could have stepped over it; the Genil looked like a shallow brook. So insignificant did the two rivers, which bear names famous in the world of history and poetry, appear, but torrential rain such as we had experienced in Barcelona would doubtless restore them.

After six days, during which the festivities continued, the Queen left Granada to visit Málaga.

Collin and I moved up to the *Fonda de los Siete Suelos*[6] which lies close to the walls of the *Alhambra,* just by the bricked-up gate through which the Moorish king Boabdil rode out when fate decreed that he should be conquered by Ferdinand and Isabella and see himself and his people thrust out of the land where for centuries they had been the masters.

Down in Granada it was still as warm as on a summer day, but up here in *Siete Suelos* it was too cool : the sun only rarely pierced through the leaves into the rooms. We lived under shady trees, with splashing fountains and rippling streams – it must be like paradise here in the burning heat of summer, but at this time of year it was not warm enough for me. The dinner table was set in the garden under the vines. The waiter ran about with his shirt sleeves turned up, thinly clad as for African heat – I put my winter coat on when I had to sit outside. The water was blessedly fresh and cold and tasted better to us than the always warm Spanish wine, but the cold water up here is melted snow from the *Sierra Nevada* and, for all its good taste, is by no means healthy. Before I had given it a thought, I felt ill. Collin came home from one of his excursions in burning sunshine with a splitting headache – he was more ill than I – went straight to bed and asked for a doctor. But where was one to be found? I rushed down to Granada. Larramendi got hold of the doctor of the Córdoba Regiment who promised to come as soon as he could. I was in such a nervous state and so weak when I got back home to the hotel that I nearly fainted. The doctor found us both very poorly and Collin had a high fever. It was a painful, long night that followed. . . .

The following day we already felt better and the day after we could again take our small trips : my walk, which became a daily enjoyment, was to the nearby *Generalife*, the summer residence of the Moorish kings, the Sultanas' shady garden with its rippling streams.

A few steps from the *Fonda de los Siete Suelos*, outside the old walls of the *Alhambra*, is a little *venta* where, under the leafy canopy of a spreading vine, peasants and townsfolk often empty their flasks of wine. A little brook with glass-clear water forms the boundary between the inn and the road. It has neither bridge nor plank and one crosses over on a couple of stepping stones. Behind the house a broad path leads to an extensive vineyard and orchard, filled with orange and pomegranate trees, with poplars and elms. Beyond this, at the end of an avenue of old cypresses and tree-high vines, lies a friendly, shining white villa : this is the *Generalife*. Here, the small gardens set on terraces still flourish with lovely, sweet-scented flowers and the clear rippling mountain streams. The place belongs to a rich Italian family who never come here but see that it is well looked after.

A couple of knocks with the iron hammer, the gate is opened and we step into a little oblong garden with flowering myrtle hedges, trimmed like our old-fashioned box borders. Clear, transparent water ripples, bubbles and hurries on its way through a long, marble pool. To the right are walls bright with myriad climbing plants, and terraces where we see a profusion of lovely, dark-red roses. To the left, an arched passage, built in Moorish style, leads to pavilions joined by arcades. All around are decorations of fantastic scrolls and inscriptions, carved and engraved in the hard porcelain walls. We are in a new *Alhambra*, not so rich or extensive as the great royal palace opposite, but more alive. A collection of portraits, among them Boabdil, also Ferdinand and Isabella, looks down on us from the walls. The garden itself blooms as in the time of the Sultanas : mighty cypresses, which once afforded shade to those proud beauties, still flourish here. One goes up from terrace to terrace by marble steps or slanting paths inlaid with small coloured stones. At the top, on the other side of the garden wall, one sees only bare, stony ground. The hill slopes up, bearing on its peak the ruins of an old Moorish fort. Gardens blossomed there once, where now only the thistly, prickly

cactus brings forth its flowers. Down below in the ravine flows the
Darro and on its further bank the ground rises gently up, with the
ruins of a monastery and with poor houses set among broad vineyards. Here once were splendid marble baths and time and again
the gardener breaks his spade on costly mosaic pavements; wild
laurel hedges lay their green branches – tokens of honour – over
hidden memories.

I was drawn to the *Generalife* more often than to the *Alhambra*
itself. Here the air was full of the scent of roses as in the poetry
of those olden days; the sound of the clear rippling water was as
it had ever been and the mighty, ancient cypresses, silent wit-
nesses of what legend and song have recorded, still stood with
their fresh branches in the air I was breathing. Here I lived so
much in the past that I would not have been surprised had figures
from the days of the Moors glided past me, in rustling damask
and glittering brocade.

Poets and historians describe the Abencerrages as the most
handsome, most chivalrous men in Granada. Their magnanimity
and philanthropy were outstanding and it is said that they were
greatly admired by all the women in the land, from the poorest
peasant to the *Alhambra*'s mighty Sultana. This aroused the
jealousy of the equally powerful Zegris, jealousy which soon became deadly enmity. When, therefore, down in Granada, by
order of the Moorish kings a tournament was to be held, but with
blunted weapons, the Zegris came with their war spears and
entered the lists against the Abencerrages, who also seized their
proper weapons. In fear and alarm the King and his court sprang
down to the field and commanded the combatants to part. The
hatred increased over the years. It happened, so the historians
recount, that four knights of the House of Zegri marched in to
King Boabdil and told him that, as evening fell, they had been
walking in the gardens of the *Generalife* and there, hidden wit-
nesses, they had seen one of the proud Abencerrages sitting hand
in hand with the loveliest of the Sultanas – they had seen and
heard a kiss. In a wild fury Boabdil commanded all the Abencerrages to be summoned to the *Alhambra*: one by one they
entered the hall which still bears their name and each and every

one was cut down and his head thrown into the marble bowl, from where the blood soon stained the water in the *Alhambra* conduits. One of the pages, who had witnessed his master's murder, escaped from the palace down on to the road where he met and warned a number of the Abencerrages on their way to answer the king's summons. They speedily turned back.

The fate of the beautiful, unfortunate Sultana was to be decided by knightly combat, the result of which would be taken as proof of God's judgement. Clothed in black, she stood in the open market place. Her four accusers, the Zegris, presented themselves, well armed, to uphold in battle and before God the truth of their story. But God sent champions for her : as it is told, they fought, they vindicated her honour and freed her – for in the fight they killed the four Zegris. . . .

It was in the gardens of the *Generalife* that I felt the first touch of winter, a puff of wind, a kiss that made the trees in a second cast their yellow leaves. From my room in *los Siete Suelos* I had gone into the sunshine which, at that moment, was strong enough to warm me up when I was freezing in the shadow-buried *Fonda*. I had only a short way to go through the avenues and when I stood on the mountain ridge looking towards Granada the sun was burning, almost scorching the dusty cacti which, with their heavy leaves, hung over the slopes. Here on a wretched patch of ground a whole gypsy family lived. The brown-skinned children ran about, nearly always naked, their matted black hair hanging over their shoulders. They were so warmed through by the sunshine that they never felt the cold. Deep down below me I saw the streets of Granada, I saw the sunlit new *Alameda*, I saw the whole fertile *campaña*, the rich *vega*. In the fields the young corn stood as fresh and green as if springtime, in the last days of summer, had suddenly overtaken winter and was in command of the earth. I looked out towards the mountains, behind which lies Málaga – the road I should soon take again. The *Sierra Nevada* raised its green terraces high over the woods and orchards; higher up, the mountain assumed wild shapes, crowned on its summit with glaciers and eternal snow. My eye followed the Darro and Genil as they flowed together, twisting their way through the fruitful valley. Suddenly, down below, a puff of smoke rose in the air, it increased and broadened out like the smoke of a forest or heath fire; it appeared in three different places, each far from the other. But it was not smoke or fire, it was dust from the highway, lifted up and carried along by a storm-wind. Round about me where I stood it was completely still, the wind had not reached here but, a few minutes later, just as I entered the *Generalife* garden, suddenly the clouds came chasing across the sun, there followed a gust of wind, whistling in the air – and the leaves fell. It was as if a giant hand was shaking the trees in the garden. It was cold. I felt as if, in the twinkling of an eye, I had been transported home to the North. I started, and hurried out of the garden as if I could thus run away from the autumn. This icy cold wind came from the south; it passed on, taking the clouds with it – and the sun went on shining.

The North had cast a snowball over into the African desert, which had thrown it back again – hence this icy wind, which was in no way tempered with the kiss of the sun. I could think of no other explanation.

If I wanted to return to summer, to be really warm through and through, I only had to go down into the streets of Granada where the air was warm and the white houses and walls reflected back the heat of the sun. The same scorching air still prevailed in the *campaña*. To get warm again, to feel again that I was in sunny Spain, I therefore went down to the city, through the gate leading to Cartuja, the Carthusian Monastery famous not only for its wealth and splendour but also for its extensive gardens. All foreigners, even the people of Granada itself, said again and again 'When you have seen *Cartuja* you have seen the best that Granada has to offer. Nowhere in the world will you see its like. You cannot go away without having seen *Cartuja*.'

The road out to the monastery was dusty and long; the sun was burning down – it was too much for me. In the whole monastery there was only a single Brother left and he showed us round. All the monks had been expelled. There was gold and marble in plenty, but it seemed to me that in Italy, especially in Rome, I had seen just as much indeed displayed with much more taste. Of all the magnificence in *Cartuja*, I have a lively recollection of only one thing, a cross painted on the white wall of one of the monastery rooms. It was impossible to see that it was only painted. I had to believe the word of the holy Brother and not the evidence of my own eyes – for they said that it was indeed a veritable cross hanging there. The door to the chapel is of ivory, mother-of-pearl and rosewood. This is the wonder which is so vaunted and for which, in beauty and splendour, the *Cartuja* is compared with the *Alhambra* and the *Generalife*.

The road went through the gypsy quarter, a hut settlement in a cactus desert; the heavy, grey-green leaves with their millions of prickly spikes made an impenetrable hedge, the red fruit blazing out from the spiked edge of the leaves. . . . In front of one of the houses sat an old dark-brown *Gitana* in a coloured skirt and with big silver rings in her ears : her grey, streaked hair fell over her almost black shoulders. She had a long bamboo stick in her hand with which she felt her way – she was blind. She could hear by our footsteps that we were not of her race; she stretched out her hand, I laid a *peseta* in it. She mumbled some words which I did not understand. Some half-naked, sunburnt children ran with bare feet right up to the prickly hedge and with a long knife cut off some of the red fruit. . . .

The sun went down as I approached the Darro. It was still and peaceful.

Between the *Alhambra*'s high walls and the *Generalife* garden, not far from the *Fonda de los Siete Suelos* and close by the little *venta*, a cart-way goes down to the city, but it is so steep that vehicles can scarcely negotiate it. An arch of the old aqueduct from the *Generalife* to the *Alhambra* forms a portal over the lane. Fig trees and flowering creeping plants hang in rich profusion on both sides over tumbledown walls. Clear water from the *Generalife* garden ripples over the broken stones. In the ruined walls and hill slopes there are many deep cavities and in front of such a hole I often saw an old couple sitting, perhaps they lived there. One day the woman was cooking over a little fire she had kindled; later I saw the two of them enjoying a cigar – that is to say one cigar, for they took turn and turn about, first the man and then the woman having a puff. There was something very conjugal in this : it could have been sketched with the inscription, 'Only one cigar, but domestic bliss', regardless of the fact that they had no roof over their heads.

The road twists steeply downwards and at every turn, whether one looks forward or back, a new picture unfolds of steep, threatening rocks, red walls and lofty towers. The road is called 'The Way Of The Dead' because by it the dead were taken down in the evening from the *Alhambra* for burial. I walked there often. The road leads to a bridge over the Darro and in the street nearby lies an old Moorish bath house which has been converted into an apartment and store-rooms for the paper factory run by our fellow-countryman, Herr Visby. The building did not, in fact, have the usual Moorish elegance, with light columns and horse-shoe windows, but was heavily built, with a lot of rococo decoration. An arched colonnade encloses a square garden in which roses, oleanders and pomegranates run wild. Water splashes and ripples there as it does everywhere in Granada.

If he had lived here Salvator Rosa[7] might have taken this 'Way of the Dead' as a setting for one of his robber scenes. It made one nervous to wander here after sunset. The tall cacti lifted their heavy leaves which seemed to peer out like heads. Darkness brooded in the deep clefts of the broken walls and the caves in the earth. Were one now to meet a couple of armed peasants or to see muffled figures bearing the dead in an open coffin, it would not need the extravagant fantasy of Don Quixote to take one back to the days of chivalry and banditry. It was a tempting spot for an assault and in fact we did see something of the sort enacted up here, albeit from the comfort of our own balcony.

A number of young men had been drinking, and rather too much, at the little *venta* near to the *Generalife* garden. Their sweethearts were with them and may indeed have been the cause of the trouble.

Collin and I were in our rooms when we heard, in the distance, a piercing scream : I thought it was the cry of an animal. It was repeated and sounded nearer and soon we realized that it was women who were giving these cries of distress. The neighbours

shut their doors and windows and so they did in the hotel. We
stepped out on to the balcony : it was pitch dark in the avenue,
only from our *fonda* a shaft of light fell across the road to the
white walls of the house opposite. Someone shrieked, 'Help!
Help! He is killing me!' and in a wild flight someone rushed past,
pursued by two others. We saw the flash of knives. The women
fled into the dark undergrowth. Deep, hoarse, male voices cursed
and swore. There was a tremendous noise and a sound of thrash-
ing – one could feel each blow! It was as if someone were beating
sacks with an enormous cudgel; the blows were so heavy that a
single one would have broken my back. It was horrible and
frightening.

The next morning the battlefield outside looked quiet and
peaceful : the sun played through the trees, the fountain splashed
and the clear stream rippled on its way, bearing with it petals of
fresh-plucked roses. There was a click of castanets; a handsome
young lad, in velvet and with well-combed hair, was dancing in
the middle of the dusty road with a girl, scarcely twelve years old.
She was clean but poorly dressed, in a cornflower-blue frock and
rose-red apron; she had a yellow dahlia in her black hair. The
dance was gracious but in the end passionate. From every balcony
they received applause and money.

A flock of holiday-clad gypsies came by, probably a whole
family, the women in loud, clashing colours and with flame-red
flowers in their shining black hair. Even the very small children,
who were being carried, all had flowers in their hair too. They
were on their way up to the *Alhambra*.

When, shortly afterwards, I went up in order to see that lovely
place once more, I and a lot of other visitors had to wait for some
time. By command of Her Majesty, the Court of Lions and the
Hall of the Two Sisters were being photographed by a famous
English photographer[8] and no one was being allowed in for fear
of disturbing him. We looked through one of the archways; the
gypsy family whom I had seen on their way, had been summoned
up here to provide human interest in the pictures. They stood and
sat in groups in the court. A couple of the babies were quite
naked; two young girls stood in dancing positions, holding

castanets. An old and incredibly ugly gypsy, with long grey hair, propped himself up against one of the slender marble columns and played the *zambomba*, a sort of kettle-drum. A fat but still quite pretty woman played the tambourine. The picture was taken more quickly than I can describe it. Perhaps I shall see it one day – but it was, I am sure, the last time I shall see the *Alhambra.*

X

From Granada to Gibraltar

We left Granada on Tuesday morning, the 21 October. Colonel
Larramendi and Visby, our two faithful friends in the ancient
city of the Moors, were there to see us off; my young friends,
Larramendi's children, were there too to shout *'Adios! Vaya
usted con Dios!'*

The diligence was a kind of omnibus with seats along the sides,
which were pretty well full up. An old grandmamma with a
crinoline took up most of the space : it was so big that it could
have provided cover for all the rest of us. She got so many kisses
that these too would have satisfied the whole company had they
been shared around. Three very lively young Spaniards were
making the journey. They were brimming over with folk-songs –
a whole treasure trove for a collector of folk melodies. While we
were still in the endless suburbs of Granada they began to sing,
every possible kind of ditty, mostly sung in peasant fashion which,
in Spain as in Italy, is rather nasal with long humming notes. For
the first three hours it was very interesting, then it became tedious,
but there was no respite. Some juicy songs were included in the
programme as I could judge from the words I understood and
from the hearty laughter with which the young men accompanied
each verse. They took no notice of old grandma : she slept or
pretended to sleep. With this cheerful singing we drove over the
campaña where, here and there, a light flickered in one of the
farmhouses or a bonfire burned in the fields.

Towards midnight we got to Loja; there we parted from our
young singers and took on new company, a whole family. The
man was tall, dark and serious with Spanish *grandeza* : he looked
very learned and was called *Catedrático*, that is to say, Professor.
His wife was an attractive child who looked about sixteen, with

large gentle eyes – and three children. We had them all in the carriage: they did everything that children can do and would not sleep without a light. The young mama therefore sat with a big lighted wax candle in her hand, which shone so that I was nearly dazzled by it, and when she wanted to sleep then the father had to hold the light, and when he wanted to sleep then the nursemaid had to hold it, and when she fell asleep and nearly dropped both candle and baby, then her neighbour blew out the light and we sat in sleep-inducing darkness. But suddenly the youngest began to scream for light and the second joined in and then the third. Everyone was woken up and the beacon was lit again.

The carriage rocked, people smoked tobacco and the young mother was sea-sick. Those were the events of the night. Outside, the air was cold and clammy. A damp mist lay over the mountains; it dispersed only when, at daybreak, we reached the summit and began the descent down to Málaga. It was deserted and barren all round. We were driving along the edge of a deep ravine; down in the narrow valleys it was still dark while we up in the heights could see every object around us clearly. The bells on the mules seemed to sound louder in this tremendous silence. We met mounted and armed police, always in pairs. At one place they had lit a fire by the roadside and, dismounted, were warming themselves.

Now the sun came out and there was the sea, broad, smooth and blue. The white flat-roofed houses of Málaga, its mighty cathedral and the high-lying Moorish castle stood out against the sky and sea. Now we could see the dried-up bed of the river Guadalmedina; we drove down and, between great, dusty cactus hedges, rolled towards the city. It was like going home to be there again, everything was so familiar to us, and in the hotel we were received like old friends.

I sat again on the balcony looking over the *Alameda*; it looked as if the same crowd of people were there as before and as if the same ships were still in harbour, but this was not so since all the Danish ships had sailed for home.

I hurried off to see Consul Scholtz and my other friends and was made very welcome everywhere. I strolled through the crowd

in the *Alameda* and along the sea-front where the surf was breaking high. I drove out to my favourite place, the Protestant
Cemetery – my thoughts had turned there when I felt so ill in the
Fonda de los Siete Suelos. The sea looked darker than when I was
here last and showed that it could be very stormy; the wind blew
strongly as at home in Denmark, the clouds gathered and there
were heavy drops of rain.

The next day there stood in the Málaga newspaper 'Winter
began yesterday'. The bad weather had begun but it would not
get worse, for otherwise there would be no truth in the lines :

> *Málaga la hechicera*
> *La de eterna primavera*
> (Enchanting Málaga with its eternal spring.)

During the past two weeks a number of English people with
chest complaints had been arriving – as sure a sign of winter here
as, at home with us, the arrival of the stork betokens spring.

The theatres had opened. They had begun with the Italian
operas, Verdi's *Rigoletto, La Traviata* and *Un Ballo in Maschera,*
and they were now going to try German music with a presenta-
tion of Flotow's opera *Martha.* So far as I could ascertain, not
one of Mozart's operas, not even his immortal masterpiece with
the real Spanish subject, *Don Juan,* had yet crossed the Pyrenees.
Flotow's *Martha* was the first revelation from Germany : his
French- and Italian-sounding melodies had arrived like the light
troops, the advance guard before the heavy brigade of the musical
army, led by the sovereigns, Mozart and Beethoven, with the
generals, Carl Maria Weber, Marschner and others.

I was present at the first performance of *Martha.* The title role
was beautifully sung by a young Polish lady, the tenor was Russian; the other singers – male and female – were from Italy. The
decorations and scenery were poor, but the voices and enuncia-
tion were good. Even so there was no applause at all during the
performance. The reason, as explained to me, was that the reigning *prima donna* had not been given a part in this opera; she was
however present in a box near the orchestra, and she would never

have forgiven her public had anyone other than herself been applauded in that house. All the same, she had a good heart – it was said that in the interval she went backstage and thanked the singers who had been so ignored by the public. . . .

The day of departure came. The steamship *Paris*, which had been delayed by storms after leaving Lisbon, arrived in the early morning and was due out the same evening on the return journey. When I was packing my things I got a surprise, a shock, in fact I was very upset indeed.

I had, naturally, left my Orders and Decorations at home in Denmark, but I had taken with me the miniature reproductions on a gold chain. Among them was the *Nordstjerne*,[1] which had belonged to Oehlenschläger.[2] Once, when I was very cast down by an unreasonably harsh criticism of my work as a writer, he had given me this medal with words of appreciation and encouragement. It always reminded me of him and was the only souvenir of him that I possessed. I had regarded it as an amulet for this journey. I had worn the chain only once in Málaga at a formal dinner; in Granada I had shown it to one of my friends and had then put it away. That was several weeks ago and now, suddenly, when I opened the box it was gone. I looked in every box and case I had, I shook every garment, but in vain. I wrote to Herr Visby in Granada about it and he had enquiries made in the two hotels in which I had stayed. Consul Scholtz put an advertisement in the 'lost or stolen' columns of the Málaga and Granada newspapers, but I never recovered the chain. The *Nordstjerne* which Oehlenschläger had worn and which he himself had given me was lost and I never saw it again. I was very sad at this loss and the thought of it still hurts me. . . .

The sun was still shining on the fort, the old *Gibralfaro*, when our Consul and I were rowed out in his boat to the steamer. Darkness fell suddenly and quickly: I preferred to go on board in daylight. Collin arrived later in the evening but in time enough for the ship's departure, which took place only about midnight. The lights in the town twinkled at us; the lighthouse was visible for a long way out. The sea was calm.

At dawn I came up on deck. The coast of Africa, with dark-

blue mountains, lay ahead of us; to the right was the Spanish
coastline with the Rock of Gibraltar at the most southerly point.
Near to it, but not in fact as near as it looked, was a whole town
of shining white houses : it was the Spanish town of Algeciras, on
the west side of Gibraltar bay, that we could see over the tang of
land which joins Gibraltar to Spain.

Our vessel glided past the flat, sandy strip of land, in under the
mighty Rock into which the sea has bored deep caves. There were
masses of screaming sea-birds. High up, tunnels have been blasted
and strong fortifications built. Eighty-pounders point their deadly
muzzles towards the sea. We shot through the water, past the
fortifications of the southern point, and then turned north into
the bay. A whole town suddenly appeared, built up on terraces :
we could see villas with terraced gardens and, finally, behind
bastions and fortified walls, the town itself rising up from the
cactus-covered rocks.

A boat came out to the steamer; all our papers were taken with
a pair of iron tongs, looked at and then returned by hand. We
were then allowed to go ashore and at the landing-stage were
given permission to stay for a few days. We were now on English
ground.

A motley crowd, a whole pattern-book of nationalities, was
milling about in and out of the low gate to the fortress, before
which stood red-coated English soldiers with blue eyes and fair
hair. Outside the gate there was a meat, vegetable and fruit
market; inside there was a vast parade ground, leading to the
town's long main street. There were Bedouins in burnouses,
Moroccan Jews in caftans, slippers and turbans, sailors of all
nationalities and some foreign visitors who were wearing long
green veils round their hats, as a protection against the fierce sun.

Our Danish Consul, Herr Mathiasen, had booked rooms for us
at the King's Arms Hotel. The hotel porter, who was at the
harbour, had been forewarned and we were soon lodged in good
English comfort. On the stairs and in the rooms one saw people
of all nationalities and tongues. At table, acquaintance was
quickly made : there were a couple of lively, friendly English
naval officers, two young Frenchmen, a German, a Russian and

two young Spaniards who had just arrived from a crocodile hunt on the Nile.

While we were still sitting at table, Consul Mathiasen came and carried us off to his hospitable house. One letter had been waiting there for me for a whole month. It was from the English Minister at Tangier, Sir John Drummond Hay,[3] who was so kind as to invite me and my companion to stay with him if we visited the African coast.

The steamship between Gibraltar and Tangier goes only once a week; it was not due out for a couple of days, so we had time to give notice of our arrival – a fisherman who often took care of mail between Gibraltar and Tangier carried my letter. All we had to do now was to make good use of the days we were to be here on the Rock of Gibraltar.

Consul Mathiasen came to take us on a very attractive tour. We drove through the mighty and awesome fortifications, along a narrow, twisting road out on to the flat tang of land which joins the Rock to the Spanish mainland. Everything was scorched and dry; here and there stood an aloe with its thick broken stem, the dust lying deep on the heavy, sword-long leaves. To the left stretched the bay over to Algeciras, to the right the open sea. On the sands over which we drove there was an encampment. The English garrison here are quartered, turn and turn about, in the town and outside under canvas, in order to accustom them to camp life.

We soon reached and crossed a barren stretch of neutral land, a gun-shot wide, on the other side of which was the first little Spanish town. It was enclosed by railings; Spanish soldiers stood at the gate.

We turned round and there before us, rising up from the sand-dunes and the sea, was the mighty perpendicular wall of rock. One could see clearly the embrasures in the galleries which have been tunnelled in the rock. Shooting practice with live ammunition was going on on the sandy isthmus; we had therefore to keep to the road and return the same way. Through the fortifications and over the walls, we came out of the town on the south side to the *Alameda* and a district with a lot of gardens. South Gibraltar lay below us. We drove past friendly-looking country places with white walls and green-painted shutters; the gardens were ablaze with trees bearing what looked like great, red sunflowers. There was a profusion of greenery and coloured climbing plants. In a villa which belonged to our Consul's mother-in-law, an Irish lady, we enjoyed refreshments and the most beautiful view over Algeciras bay to the town and hills, and round to Tarifa and the African coast. But there was an even grander view to come. From the southernmost point of the Rock the carriage-way turns towards the north-east and shortly afterwards comes to an end; from there we climbed on foot as high as we could get on the scorched rock, which was weathered by the sun and the sea mists.

Passing soldiers and cannons, we reached this impressive solitude. Wild cucumbers grow over the rocks; deep down below us we could see the dark-blue, almost ink-black water, with foaming white waves. A fisherman lay in his boat down there; seabirds flew over him into the deep crevices in the rock. Many ships had sought shelter here and awaited a favourable wind to pass through the Straits out into the Atlantic. We could see the whole way round, from the dark mountains to the north beyond the bay of Málaga, along the coast and out over the endless Mediterranean; to the south rose the African mountains. It is only about fifteen miles from here over to Ceuta, the Spanish town on the African coast; it was so distinct in the thin, clear air that one could easily pick out individual buildings. The contour of the mountains stood out clearly, one range behind the other.

Also with Consul Mathiasen, who obtained permission for us from the Governor, we saw, another day, the impregnable fortifications, all blasted into the rock. Through a small, rather built-up square, where a lot of the garrison live with their families, we were taken, escorted by two soldiers, into prison-like vaults. Everything was locked and barred again behind us. We were in total darkness, but suddenly stepped out into open galleries with the clear sky above us and the Rock itself as a wall with embrasures. It was a tiring climb right up to the signal station at the top of the Rock. The way down took us past an enormous rock cavern, in which peculiar stalactite formations and unfathomable depths are of great interest. There is a legend, a popular belief, that this cavern stretches right under the Straits and comes out on the African coast. It is thought that the apes found their way over here through this undersea tunnel. Many skeletons of these animals are found in the cavern, for the apes bury their dead themselves. When Collin was there, the Governor happened to be visiting the place with a party and blue lights were lit, in which the curious shapes and stalactite figures stood out like trolls. Towards the north-west there can still be seen the remains of a kind of fort from the time of the Moors, but they have been, as it were, incorporated into the later walls and fortifications which extend from the top to the bottom of the Rock. In Gibraltar one is under lock and key and one is especially aware of this at sunset. A signal shot is fired, the gates are locked and all communication with the outside world is broken off until sunrise, when a cannon shot gives the order for the gates to be opened. If one does not remember this then one is not conscious of any restriction: the long, gas-lit streets are thronged with people of all nations, Turks, Arabs, Englishmen and Frenchmen, military bands play, the theatre begins. At that moment they were presenting an opera, one of the latest, *Moreto*, with music by a Spaniard : it was being very well received.

We had grey, rainy weather for half a day, like a northern autumn, but this was most unusual. Gibraltar's whole winter is confined to a couple of such blowy, grey, damp days. By Christmas, I was told, it is already spring here and one can see fresh green and early flowers.

The next day we had lovely warm sunny weather and it was the 1 November. Collin crawled about on the rocks, looking for snails and other specimens for his collection. I went for a stroll with a cheerful young Frenchman. We walked towards the *Alameda* and so came first to the cemetery. It lies under the walls, close by the south gate of the town. Fig trees cast their shade over the graves, dark cypresses and flowering bushes providing some variety. There were tall hedges with big, bell-shaped flowers, rather like the white *Calla* :[4] they grow all round in the gardens and are used by the ladies when they are going to a ball. For the first hour the flowers keep their original colour, but as the night wears on they turn lilac and in the early morning they are red. We were soon on the *Alameda*, which looked very inviting with its trees, bushes and flowers. Here one can feel a fresh sea breeze and from here one can look out over to the broad bay filled with boats and ships, out to Algeciras and the bare, stony cliffs which are the end of Europe. . . .

XI

A Visit to Africa

In the early morning of 2 November the steamer left Gibraltar for Tangier. Collin and I had already gone on board when we had the pleasure of seeing our friend, Herr Consul Mathiasen, yet once more. He came to bring us greetings from his wife and a young man not known to us – his youngest son who had been born early that morning, a new inhabitant for the Rock of Gibraltar.

The crew of the steamer were almost all Moors. The porter from the hotel handed us over to one of them, the second mate. The vessel was very small and bobbed up and down with the waves. We steered across the bay towards Algeciras, then went along the Spanish coast, which was bare and rocky, right in under Tarifa. Black rock masses rose up from the sea with the surf breaking over them. The whole of this southerly point of Europe is wild mountain country, scorched and desolate. The town of Tarifa is hidden behind bare cliffs; only an old grey-black lighthouse stood out, encircled by screaming birds. Africa, as we steamed towards it from Tarifa in the direction of Tangier, looked smiling and fertile. Up behind Ceuta the landscape looked impressive with three ranges of mountains rising up, one behind the other : one of them looked jagged and indented like *Montserrat* near Barcelona. But as the coast stretches towards Tangier, out of the Straits and towards the Atlantic, it becomes lower, with green hills not unlike the north coast of Sjælland. Tangier now came into sight, with white walls, flat-roofed houses and a chalk-white fortress at the highest point. Behind the town there appeared to be a foretaste of the golden sands of the desert and over it rolled a caravan of laden camels. There is no harbour here, no shelter against the rolling sea, even the long mole was destroyed by the Europeans before they abandoned their occupation of Tangier. The steamer stopped a fairly long way out and cast anchor. Some boats came quickly out to us, with half-naked, sunburnt Moors who swarmed up the side of the ship, shouting and gesticulating. I expected someone to meet us from Drummond Hay's house, but saw no one.

Our mate secured one of the boats for us and immediately we and our belongings were more or less pulled down into it and rowed off at great speed towards the shore; great waves were rolling in, breaking high up on the sand. A dozen or so caftan-clad Moroccan Jews sprang into the water and waded out to us. One snatched a trunk, another a portmanteau and a third ran off with our umbrellas – it was just like pillage. They ignored our shouts and protestations. One seized me by one leg, a second grabbed my other leg and before I knew what was happening I was on the shoulders of a third and thus, lifted up on high, I, Collin and an English traveller were borne safely to dry land, between fishing boats drawn up on the beach and spread-eagled, half-sleeping Moors. Some of them turned over and dozed again, others got up and with a whole flock of naked, screaming children followed us to the open outer gate of the town. We stood there as if we had been transported to Damascus or another of the famous cities of *A Thousand and One Nights*. Here, in the open hall, sat men with turbans and long beards, looking like the seven wise men – except that there were only six of them and I cannot vouch for their wisdom, since I did not understand their language. We were in the Customs Hall and were required to open our baggage. I knew neither Moroccan nor Arabic; I therefore simply said the magic words, 'The English Ambassador', and that was enough. We were well treated and given permission to proceed and that we did, escorted by a flock of half-naked barbarians – but after all, we were on the Barbary coast, in the country from which in olden days the pirates set sail – as they did from Tunis, Algiers and Tripoli for example – to indulge in robbery and murder. Our escorts shouted and jabbered all together : they had seized our baggage and, like the Jews who had carried us ashore, each one demanded his reward. We went through another town gate, even more narrow than the one out to the harbour, and were now walking between the white walls of houses, hot with the sun, each with a low door and hole in the wall which served as a window. The women we met drew their sack-like robes the more closely around them and glided past like shadows. Some mules and laden camels completely blocked the street, which straggled as best it might between the houses and up past the mosque. The door stood open: we dared to look in but not to stop – the place was too holy for Christian eyes.

A young Moor took us to the residence of the English Minister, but the whole family were in the country at their estate, Ravens-rock, which looks out towards the Atlantic, about four miles from Tangier. In the meantime we met Mr Green, the Secretary at the English Legation.[1] He knew that we were expected but assured us that my letter had not arrived. We later discovered that the fisherman who was bringing it had gone first to Tarifa from Gibraltar and only three days after our arrival did he deliver the letter saying we were coming.

Horses and mules were quickly brought for us and our baggage. There was no question of driving: there are no carriages in Tangier and the streets are like dried river beds: one has to proceed over stones, rubbish and bits of broken brick. Nearly all the houses have only one opening which is both door and window and which can serve equally as counter or workshop. Traders and workmen squatted inside: they were mostly Moroccan Jews in long dressing-gowns, with sashes round the waist. On the street itself we saw a lot of Arabs in the white burnous. The water sellers had little on but a shirt and were very strange-looking, with brass ornaments in their coal-black, bushy hair. They come into Tangier from hundreds of miles inland, in order to earn a little money by selling water, which they carry on their backs in great goatskin bags with the hair still on outside. The water seeps through the skin so that their backs are always completely wet, with drops of water running down their dark-brown limbs. Half-naked, sunburnt boys either pressed around us or lay outside the entrance to the house, playing some game with sticks. Moorish women glided by aloof from everything: almost shrouded in hessian, they looked like walking mill-sacks. The western gate of the town is low and narrow. The twisting lane up to it was crowded with people and animals; it was market day. Just outside the walls we had to go through a whole encampment of Bedouins and Arabs, lying with their camels in the deep sand. A couple of young Moorish lads led our mules. Mr Green escorted us. We rode off through the picturesque heath, where enormous cacti grew in profusion. We passed some deserted villas, where the orange trees had grown into a thick copse and rode on between wooded slopes with laurel hedges and thickets of dwarf palms. Our road, if it could be called a road, in some parts was like the rough, unpaved streets of Tangier, in others a narrow moorland path. It led us through an Arab's country dwelling and his family cemetery; now we were in a plantation of Spanish rushes and then again we were out on the heath. Deep below us was the rolling sea, behind us over the shining, dark-green woodland, we could see the town of Tangier and the whole coastline, with an ever-moving border of foam-white surf. Mr Green told us that, nine years ago, a lion had roamed about here. Drummond Hay, with a lot of the local people, had hunted him but without success. At length one of the Moors spotted him : the man was so terrified that he stood stockstill, deathly pale, and could not utter a word. There were plenty of wild animals here. Mr Green said we should probably see wild boar and porcupines and perhaps at night hear the cries of the jackals which came into the garden. We reached the house after an hour's ride. Ravensrock, big and shining white like a palace, stood surrounded by green trees, high over the sea. Houses for the various servants, wash-houses, stables and so on, all with flat white roofs, were scattered around the garden, which was in fact land reclaimed from the heath. Outside there was a wilderness of flowering myrtles, great bushes with fruit like strawberries, dwarf palms, and wild orange trees, which had been allowed to remain when the garden was being laid out. All the domestic staff, women included, were Moors. The head servant, Hussein, was a handsome man with a stately turban and a white burnous with black stripes which any lady in one of our European cities might have worn. He came out with two young Moors, Hamed and Boomgrais, in white plush trousers and red fez : they helped us dismount and took the mules off to the stables. Sir John Drummond Hay, a man with a wise, friendly face, received us so kindly that we felt at once that we were welcome. Lady Drummond Hay and their two young daughters greeted us in Danish. It was strange to hear our dear mother tongue on the African coast, near to the mighty, rolling Atlantic Ocean.

The room to which I was shown had the most beautiful view. To the right, over the garden and the wooded, green coast, one could see behind Tangier the high blueish hills by Ceuta and beyond that the open Straits leading to the Mediterranean, with an endless traffic of steamers and sailing ships. Straight across was the Spanish coast, from the Rock of Gibraltar to Tarifa, the bay of Trafalgar and the mountains up towards Cadiz. The Atlantic stretched out into infinity to the west.

VIEW FROM RAVENSROCK. Sketch by Andersen.

It was lovely here in the evening. The lighthouse at Tarifa seemed so near, and now and then one caught a glimpse of the beam from the distant Trafalgar lighthouse. A full moon shone over the broad, rolling sea; the green-blue air was immeasurably translucent. The moon sailed through the heavens and the stars themselves seemed to be rolling like spheres through endless space.

Outside, everything about us was new and strange, but inside the house we found English comfort and the most kind-hearted people, whose sole thought was to make our stay with them as happy as possible. I enjoyed untroubled, unforgettable days here – a new and rich page in the story of my life.

Lady Drummond Hay, one of those calm, noble, feminine natures, is a daughter of the late Danish Consul-General, Carstensen, in Tangier. There was much talk of friends and relations in our beloved Denmark; Danish melodies were played on the piano. The two young daughters of the house sat with us: Alice, who was born in Copenhagen and Louise, born in Tangier. They knew my stories in an English translation. The French edition, published in Geneva, which includes 'The Marsh-King's Daughter',[2] a story in which the scene changes between Denmark and Africa, was in the bookcase. I autographed this volume and wrote a verse to the children.

We walked out of the garden into the country, covered with wild flowers and a glory of heather: there was a wealth of different varieties which would have graced the most select hothouse in Europe. Dwarf palms spread their green fans into a bouquet, as does the bracken with us. Myrtles and laurels formed a thick copse. There was a splendid view out over the whole country, far away to the south-east. The snow-capped Atlas Mountains rose on the horizon like the Alps. Over us flew a noisy flock of ravens. There are so many of them here that they have given the place its name – Ravensrock.

The Moors tell a story about the ravens; I heard it from Drummond Hay, who suggested that I should sometime use it.

The Moors believe that, when they are hatched out, the ravens are white, and they recount with much vivacity how astounded Father Raven was when the fledgling crept out of the shell – and was white. 'What is this?' said Father and he looked at himself : not a single white feather could he find on his body, but the baby was undoubtedly white. He looked at Mother Raven, but not a white feather was to be found on her either. And so he addressed himself to Mother and demanded an explanation.

'I do not understand,' she said, 'but just be patient and it will all come right.'

'I shall fly away from here,' he said, 'Caw, Caw!' and away he flew. Mother stayed with the child. Father was as angry as he could possibly be, but after he had been flying for some time he began to think, 'Did I really see aright? I must go back and have another look,' and when he came and looked, the white fledgling had turned grey. 'It is not white,' he said, 'but all the same, one cannot call it black! Neither Mother nor I look like that!' and off he flew again. But he came back once more and this time the young bird had turned black.

'Just be patient and the truth will out.' This is the moral and this the Father believed ever after.

In the neighbourhood, under pines and among orange trees heavy with fruit, one of Tangier's wealthiest Jews had his country estate : this and a few Moorish huts were the only places near. A footpath, very seldom used, wound through the scrub down to the sea. It was on this path that the famous lion had first been seen some years ago. I thought of this when here one day I saw a large, tawny animal. I will not deny that for a moment I was terrified – it was in fact only a dog, but dogs are not always exactly harmless here. However I encountered neither ichneumon nor wild boar, although one had recently broken into the garden. A porcupine ran across the path where I was walking; on my way home I found one of its long quills. I now use it as a pen-holder.

There was something very fascinating in wandering further and further from all signs of habitation, something stimulating in not knowing where one would get to and what one might meet. Everything was so new and strange, but always one could hear the sound of the sea; the foreshore was strewn with stones, licked flat by the waves, coloured shells – mussels, conches and others.

6   Sir John Drummond Hay, PC, KCB, GCMG.

8 The former synagogue of Santa Maria la Blanca, Toledo.

7 The Giralda tower, Seville.

It was very deserted down there and yet teeming with life, the life and movement of the ocean. . . .

We were also to see something of life in Tangier. Drummond Hay was moving back into town with his family. The mules set off ahead in long caravans, loaded with baggage and kitchen equipment. Late in the afternoon we left romantic Ravensrock with our charming host. It was the first summer that the family had spent there; previously they had spent that part of the year in an old Moorish villa near to Tangier. We rode close by it; the garden was remarkable for its wealth of oranges and roses, which virtually looked after themselves now that the friendly careful hands had gone away. We returned by the road on which we had gone out to Ravensrock, riding between the tall bamboo reeds, past the Moorish house with its silent cemetery and up again between the high laurel hedges and the palm thickets. The ground became more and more uneven; the rest of the party were riding ahead of me and were soon out of sight. For myself I could not make out what was supposed to be the road or path, I had to leave that to the mule, but it must go a little faster, so I smacked it with a laurel branch and it increased its pace. I am no horseman, although I managed to keep my seat, but the animal knew well enough that I was not the master of creation and with this happy thought it got very sportive. The sun went down and it was suddenly evening. The deep valley lay in darkness, some bonfires were lit on the hillside and the moon shone.

Just outside Tangier, by the cactus-grown dunes, a whole caravan of camels lay in the sand. A single one lifted his head in the air and moved his long neck, the others appeared to be asleep. A fire was burning with pungent smoke, down in the deep town moat. We rode through the low, narrow gate where a couple of Arabs ran ahead of us with lighted torches up the narrow, break-neck lane. Over stones and gravel we proceeded into the street where the foreign consuls live. The French, Spanish and English Powers are represented here. Sir John Drummond Hay takes precedence, perhaps because he is the English Resident Minister for the Kingdom of Morocco. As it was now after sunset, all the flags had been taken down but during the day two flags flew over

E

his Residence, the English and the Danish because, since his father's death, Drummond Hay had been Danish Consul-General here.

We were in an old house, surrounded by high walls: it was flat-roofed and had balconies overlooking the garden. The door was firmly locked and bolted. Inside it was very comfortable and well arranged. The staircase and corridors were adorned with the skins of lions, panthers and tigers and collections of Moorish jars, spears, sabres and rifles. There were valuable saddles and saddle-cloths, most of them gifts which Sir John Drummond Hay had received when he visited the Emperor of Morocco.*

In the sitting-room, which was next to a by no means inconsiderable library, there were many paintings and engravings, among them more than one well-known place and portrait from home, from Denmark. Two valuable silver candelabra, a gift from King Oscar of Sweden, stood in one corner of the room and in the other corner was a porcelain vase given to Drummond Hay by the Danish King, Christian VIII. When the windows were closed one recognized every blind as of Danish make; on them were painted views of Frederiksborg, Frederiksberg and Rosenborg Castles. I could have believed that I was in a Danish room, in the land of Denmark.

There was every English comfort inside the room, even a fireplace. From the balcony one looked over the little garden, where a few oleander bushes were flowering among the same colour-changing bell-flowers that I had seen in the cemetery in Gibraltar. A tall palm tree lifted its crown in the moonlit, blue-green air and gave the view its especial foreign feeling. White-crested waves rolled in from the sea and the lighthouse at Tarifa, on the coast of Europe, twinkled at us as we sat in a cosy little circle in the handsomely furnished but very comfortable room. Drummond Hay told us about the country and its people, about his journey to Morocco and his sojourn in Constantinople.

There hung on the wall a portrait of the most beautiful Sultana of Mahmud II, the present Sultan's grandfather.[3] To get

* Western Barbary, its wild tribes and savage animals, by John Drummond Hay, London 1844. H.C.A.

a portrait of a Sultana sounds unbelievable and this picture indeed had its own romantic history.

The Emperor had a little dwarf of uncommonly ugly appearance, but he was blessed with so many freakish fancies that he well amused His Imperial Majesty. When one day he had particularly amused his Lord, he said, 'And what reward will you give me, Master?'

'I will give you whichever of my wives you are able to kiss,' said the Sultan.

'All very well, but I cannot reach them,' said the dwarf, 'and they will laugh.'

'That is your business,' answered the Sultan and asked for his pipe. The most beautiful of all his wives brought it, knelt and handed it to him; then the dwarf jumped up, put his arms round her neck and kissed her. 'I will give you money,' said the Sultan, 'but her I will not give you!'

'The Sultan will not break his word!' said the dwarf.

'Very well – she is yours,' answered the Sultan, 'but from this hour henceforth you shall never dare again to set foot within the gates of this seraglio.' The beautiful Sultana had to follow the dwarf. She was filled with shame and anger.

'You have got your will,' she said, 'but now I will have mine! I will be free as the Christian women are free: I will drive out when I please, I will come home when I please. I will plague you, I will torment you!' And that she did, in every possible manner and when a French painter came that way, she let him paint her picture. That is how it happened.

It was midnight before I went to my room. I did not feel sleepy or in need of rest. I could have sat for a long time thinking my own thoughts and looking up into endless space, compared with which the deepest sea is a shallow lake. I heard the Muezzin intone his watchman's song, 'Prayer is better than sleep! God is great!' The sea murmured, singing its eternal song. I lay down and closed my eyes in this Moslem city.

Tangier is the old Roman city of *Tingis*, in the western part of what was then known as Mauretania. In the eighth century it was conquered by the Moors and in the fifteenth century by the

Portuguese who, two hundred years later, handed it over to England as part of the dowry of one of their princesses.[4] One can read all this in any encyclopaedia, but it is always useful to know something about the place one is in. Armed with these facts we went out the next day, escorted by the most trusty servant of the house, Hussein. We were to see the sights of the town and, in addition, would be taken to one of the Jewish shops which had the biggest selection of Moorish wares, such as studs, tie-pins, and brooches, things one could take home to Denmark as souvenirs from Tangier. Later in Paris I found exactly the same things in a Turkish shop and when I asked if they came from Tangier, the shop-owner told me that they were all made in Paris and could be sold there for half the price demanded in Africa. Vast quantities of these goods were exported from France to Algiers, Oran and all the Mediterranean African cities. But bought in these places they were nevertheless souvenirs of Africa.

Hussein led us through a crowd of Jews and Moors. They gave way when he made a sign with his hand – here came persons of consequence, friends or relations of the English Ambassador. We visited a couple of caravanserais, heavy, clumsy buildings, though quite in Moorish style. The courtyards and arcades were filled with Arabs selling corn and chickens; their unladen donkeys huddled close together, resting themselves. It was almost impossible to get through : every inch of the courtyard was occupied and a lot of women, swaddled in their sack-like garments, spread themselves out among the asses and the corn. They turned towards us and glanced at us with one eye, the other completely hidden in the top of the sack.

At the town gate the crowd had, for a moment, come to a complete standstill; camels, donkeys, people old and young, were all pressed together. Some wanted to get out, others wanted to get in and they were all screaming and shouting. Finally we managed to slip through. A fire had been lit in the dried-up moat; its thick, black smoke licked the walls. They were slaughtering down there and it did not look very clean, with lumps of meat hanging in the sunshine, dripping blood. Before us in the sand lay laden camels; we saw another large convoy starting out on their journey and were told they were going to Tetuan. Some of the men with them were heavily armed and carried long muskets. The road out there was not safe.

All round where we were standing a lot of cooking was going on. One could both see and smell the fish being grilled. Some young women were sitting on the sand, enjoying this delicacy, with their faces uncovered. When they saw us they turned their heads away, but I could see that they had lovely eyes. A negro with great silver rings in his ears was strutting around, looking impressive; water-carriers with amulets in their wild, bushy hair were arriving with filled water-sacks, while a crowd of Moors sat in a circle and listened to a story-teller, who struck a tambourine all the time he was speaking. The listening faces were a picture.

We walked over the pathless common to the Jewish cemetery, which was not enclosed but lay like a field of flat gravestones, each with a Hebrew inscription. Here the women assemble on the Sabbath, adorn the graves with lighted candles and sit and talk, or begin to sing, to the accompaniment of stringed instruments. The view from there over the bay was very lovely. While we stood there, a long caravan passed in procession along the seashore, where the waves, white-crested, rolled up on to the sand. We followed after it, along a deep path between towering dusty cacti and fig trees. Down by the sea the surf was breaking high over the ruined pier and we got a wetting. We had to go on for some way, crawling or walking as best we could over clods of earth and bits of broken wall and then to climb up again where we could find a foothold until, finally, we reached an opening in the walls. This opening led into a tannery or slaughter-house – piggery is perhaps the most appropriate word. We were again in one of the dry, break-neck streets; from there we went into a narrow lane or alley where there was a place with a considerable selection of embroidered cushions, slippers, studs and brooches for sale. Once inside the low outer door, the house had a very inviting appearance : one stood in a paved courtyard surrounded by slender pillars; a staircase inlaid with porcelain tiles led up to an open corridor with small rooms leading off – a complete bazaar, overflowing with gold-embroidered velvet things and

articles of Moroccan leather and metal. There was a scent of
rose-oil, musk and myrrh. The young Jewish girl who showed us
round was very attractive. Her mama was in a large edition –
she could have sat as a model for Judith, that is to say, Judith
in her old age, sitting and telling her grandchildren the story of
Holofernes.

Friday is a holy day for the Moors and on that day the gates
of Tangier are closed as long as prayers are being said in the
mosques. Collin did not know this and, after our trip round the
town, had gone out on an excursion. In the afternoon he came
back, went from gate to gate but could not get in. In his wanderings he came to the Jewish cemetery; the women had lit candles
on the graves and were sitting and singing. An old Jew showed
him a pathway up to the castle, where the Pasha lives, and told
him that only by that way could he slip into the town at that
time, for from the castle a little wicket down into the town was
left open. Collin managed to get back to us this way, while
prayers were still being read in the mosques.

I also was brave enough to venture out into the town and
country without a guide. No one gave me the evil eye, indeed a
couple of Jews were all too attentive. They swept the small Arab
children aside, although they were really not in my way. One
Jew, in poor clothes, smiled all over his face and insisted on taking me into a side-street. I asked him what there was to see. 'A
Jew's house,' he said, nodding his head and making humble
gestures. I was curious and followed him into one of the narrow
alleys. We were quite alone; he wanted me to go still further up
this cul-de-sac and I became uneasy, wondering whether he was
to be trusted. The man looked honest enough, for all his poverty,
but I had a lot of money on me. However – everything around
seemed to promise an adventure. He stopped by a low door in
the wall, took a step down, stood for a moment beckoned and I
followed him. We came into a little stone-paved court, where a
grubby, elderly Jewess was bustling about. A few steps up a broad
stairway led to a little open room; here lay a pale young woman
with a blanket over her and a baby at her breast.

'A Jew's wife, a Jew's child!' said the man, laughing and

jumping about. He took the baby and held it out to me, so that
I could see that it was a real son of Abraham. I had to give it a
mite. The wife took the cushion she was lying on and gave it to
me and I sat down. The man kissed his pale, pretty wife, kissed
the child and looked very happy. The furniture seemed to consist
only of a few rags and a large pitcher.

The following day I had the opportunity of seeing another
kind of wealth in another Jewish house. Through Drummond
Hay, one of the very rich Jews had invited me to see his home,
to see how one of the most well-to-do of Tangier's Jews lived. He
came to fetch me himself, because Drummond Hay, with the
English Consul and other friends, had gone off on a hunting
expedition, in which I had neither the skill nor desire to take
part. More than a hundred people would be there to hunt or act
as beaters. Jonas Collin was mounted on a splendid Arab horse,
a present from the Emperor of Morocco : it had a pedigree
which named five hundred ancestors. The party went off at a
gallop.

The Jewish merchant, dressed in European clothes like myself,
took me to his house which was in an alley-way just as small as
the one where I had visited the poor Jew the day before. The
house itself, seen from the outside, did not look very much better.
There was a square grating in the wall and a low door. But when
I crossed the threshold into the little forecourt, it was all very
different. The floor and the stairways were paved with porcelain
tiles, the walls seemed to be of highly polished stone, the rooms
were high and airy, with open colonnades out to the courtyard.
The light fell from above. Inside sat the young wife, dressed in
her costly bridal gown – presumably so that I could see it. No
Eastern princess could have been more magnificently dressed. I
had only seen the like in *A Thousand and One Nights*, when I
roamed Baghdad with Harun al Rashid, seeking adventure.

She was wearing a green velvet skirt, richly embroidered with
gold. It was open, with an underskirt of white silk; she had a
long, red, silk sash, worked in gold thread and a brocade bodice
with many buttons and each button was a pearl. A golden veil
hung like wings down over her bare arms, which were covered

with costly bracelets, and her fingers were covered with rings.
Her hair, in accordance with Jewish custom, had been cut but
artificial plaits hung down from the blue silk scarf, twined round
her head like a turban, in the centre of which, on her brow,
sparkled a great jewel. Her earrings were so massive that they
looked like small stirrups. She was really a splendid sight and so
young and beautiful, with coal-black eyes and shining white teeth.
Her husband turned her round on the floor so that I could see
her from all sides. She spoke Arabic to him and a few words in
Spanish to me. They both seemed very happy, but even more so
was their little three-year-old daughter who stood there in velvet
and gold and laughingly offered me her hand and mouth – but
she put the latter to full use only when cake and orange liqueur
were brought.

The wife's brother arrived with two elderly ladies of the family.
They were not in their bridal array, but their clothes were rather
striking.

The bible was produced, with the text in Hebrew and English,
and they were much impressed that I – like every schoolboy in
our grammar schools – could read the first verse of *Genesis* in
Hebrew.[5]

My friendly host escorted me home again, but the way there
took us past another house, which belonged to his sister and
brother-in-law and he wanted me to see this too. Here the inner
courtyard was covered by a glass roof, resting on green columns
which lifted it up over all three storeys of the house, thus forming
a great hall, with lovely carpets on walls and floors. There were
small open cabinets, some filled with household articles and one
with Hebraic books, manuscripts and biblical pictures, which
invited one to stay there and relax, read and browse.

The lady of the house, no longer very young and dressed in
plain, dark clothes with a becoming, swathed head-dress, received
me very kindly. There were several other ladies and some children
there too. They spoke only Arabic but the husband, who soon put
in an appearance, knew some English. One of the small Jewish
boys was much amused by my visit, hiding his face in the curtains
and behind the ladies' skirts and bursting into peals of laughter.

He was much embarrassed when I drew him out and asked him his name and anything else I could think to ask. His mother translated my questions for him and prompted him when he could not think of the answers. I noticed afterwards that he stood in a corner on his toes and stretched his arms up in the air to show the other children how tall I was. The little comedian was called Moses : he was an attractive boy.

When we came out into the street we saw a number of Jews, one of them dressed all in red silk. A little negro boy came along in a shining white coat, gold-embroidered scarf and with a silver bracelet on his dusky arm. One could see that he was very proud of his appearance. I asked if there was anything special on today and was told that both the Jews and the Moslems were celebrating some festival.

Late in the afternoon our hunters returned. Collin was busy until late at night, skinning the heads of some of the animals they had shot, since he wanted the skulls. He also brought two live tortoises home and they were with us for the rest of our journey; they were for several months without food or drink and reached Copenhagen alive.

After I had gone to bed I was suddenly disturbed by a frightful drumming sound. There was the most terrible noise in the streets all round the house. I got up and asked what was going on and was told that it was the Africans in the town who were drumming away : they must be holding some festival or celebrating a wedding. But the next day we were told that the devil had got into a woman and had to be drummed out. That hobgoblins and trolls cannot bear the sound of a drum is an old belief way up in the North; now I learnt here that his satanic majesty the devil does not like drum-music either.

During the morning there was the sound of chanting in the narrow streets outside the Residence, the word Mahomet being constantly repeated. From the balcony over the garden wall I could see six Moors bearing on their shoulders a coffin wrapped in a red shawl, a sign that it was the burial of a woman – the coffins of men are quite unadorned. A great crowd of people followed through the narrow alley-ways to the mosque.

After dinner Sir John was to take Collin and me up to the castle to present us to the Pasha, who was expecting us. We would get some impression of life up there but, because of our visit, the harem would be moved into inner rooms. His Majesty, the reigning Emperor of Morocco, had, I heard, only a few hundred wives; his father, on the other hand, even when he was in his seventieth year, had eight hundred concubines and every tenth day had sent to him a fresh young girl. How many the present Pasha of Tangier in fact had, I do not know.

We went into the town, up between high walls and fortifications, to the castle. In the outer court the whole guard was drawn up on our arrival: their uniform was the burnous, bare feet in gold, Moroccan leather slippers, turbans and drawn swords. The officer of the watch shook hands with us and in the open door we saw the Pasha himself, a powerful, handsome man of about fifty. He also had bare feet in leather slippers and was rather splendidly dressed in a fine white burnous, with a turban of finest muslin. Drummond Hay presented us and his two small daughters who had accompanied us, and we were received with much cordiality and European courtesy. The Pasha shook hands with us and led us into the tile-paved court, which was reminiscent of the *Alhambra*, except that the pillars there had horseshoe arches and here had Greek capitals.

Two high-ranking Moroccan officers were in attendance. We were given chairs to sit on, but the Pasha himself took his place on a cushion on the floor, which was covered with beautiful carpets. The Pasha and Drummond Hay spoke Arabic, which seemed to be the only language spoken here. Tea was brought and we each had two large cups; I felt as if I were in a warm bath. We were offered a third cup, but I asked Drummond Hay to rescue us and to say that it was against our religion to drink three cups. We were thus excused. Very good sugar biscuits were served with the tea. We were then taken on a tour through the dark, twisting corridors of the palace, past small, mysterious alcoves and tiled bathrooms, into a little orange grove. At the top of the wall were some small, gridded windows; one of the officers touched Collin's arm and whispered, 'Beautiful eyes!' And indeed from high up, beautiful eyes were looking down at us – it was the Pasha's harem. Poor little doves in a dovecote! Cooing softly no doubt – but doubtless as cross-grained as doves can be.

The Pasha offered us horses to ride down into the town but we preferred to walk; he escorted us to the outer gate of the castle, where he offered his hand and bade us a very friendly farewell.

Every ten days a warship goes from Algiers to France, calling at Oran, Gibraltar, Tangier, Cadiz and other places. The ship was due here early in the morning of 9 November, but there was no sign of it as yet. We were going on it to Cadiz.

It was Sunday. The population of Tangier consists of Moors and Jews. The few Catholics and Protestants here have, naturally, neither church nor chapel; Sunday devotions must be observed in the family sitting-room and in one's own heart. Down in the garden-room, a cloth was spread over the table and the bible and prayer book laid on it. Drummond Hay read aloud for us a couple of psalms and the Gospel for the Day. The atmosphere was very reverent in this quiet, unpretentious church service.

In a few hours I should leave this home that I had found in a strange, distant part of the world; I should bid farewell to people who, in the short time we had been together, had sought only to make us happy. It was uncertain that we should meet again in this world; it was certain that I should not again visit the coast of Africa.

We could see the steamer approaching; it was the French warship *Titan*; soon it lay at anchor in the bay. The servants collected our baggage, Hussein and Boomgrais went ahead and Drummond Hay took us down to the boat. I always dislike partings and I felt depressed. One more handshake and we heard his warm farewell. From the ship we could see Lady Drummond Hay and the two daughters standing on the balcony of the house, waving their handkerchiefs; we waved our hats. Our boatman rowed vigorously; the sun went down and it was suddenly evening as we pulled in by the rope-ladder of the ship.

From the deck we looked once more across the water to

Tangier's white walls and flat roofs. The lights twinkled in the town. I felt very sad.

The time we had spent on the Moroccan coast had been so far the most interesting part of our journey.

XII

Cadiz

We were on a big, well-manned vessel, with cannon on both sides.
It would have put up a good fight against pirates had there been
any around. It was not very well equipped for passengers, but
the officers' quarters up on deck were comfortable and well
furnished. There was even an attractive little library; I found a
young officer there deep in *A Thousand and One Nights*, but he
was reading it in Arabic. It was a little after seven when the ship
was set in motion; the moon was not yet up, it was fairly dark. I
went early to my cabin and fell asleep, but woke with a sudden
jolt. The ship lay still; the engines had stopped, but I could hear
the steam whistling in the funnel. It was not yet half-past one.
People were tumbling about over my head, orders were being
given, there was a commotion: something unusual must have
happened. I jumped out of my bunk and ran up on deck. The
ship was listing to one side; a great many of the crew were leaning over the railing. I asked what had happened but it was some
time before I got a reply; finally someone told me that we had
run aground. There was no sign of land, the sky was star-clear,
the sea fairly calm. The sailors took no further notice of me, they
all had enough to do. We were out in the Atlantic off Trafalgar.
I had woken Collin and he too now came up on deck. A few
minutes later the ship was already moving again, pulling out
backwards from the soft ground, but I could not now sleep. The
paddles hit the water with a resounding smack, as we drove our
way over the corner of the great ocean which rolled in mighty
waves beneath us. At half-past four we cast anchor off Cadiz,
but we still had several hours to wait before the health authorities,
who were not very vigilant, would deign to put in an appearance,
take the Captain's papers and allow us to go ashore.

The sun rose; Cadiz lay before us, shining white with flat-roofed houses, which looked as if they were hewn out of chalk. The whole bay was crowded with vessels and we lay a fair distance out. One boat after another came alongside our steamer and waited in order to capture passengers. Standing-room on deck got smaller and smaller because a tremendous cleaning-up had begun. The crew were scrubbing and washing down; even in the engine-room there was major cleaning, as we could see from above. The stokers and firemen down there had stripped down and were soaping each other and pouring bucket after bucket of water over each other – both as a help and for amusement.

At last we saw the red and yellow Spanish flag flying from a boat which brought the health authorities, and we were given permission to go ashore. I was surprised that here in Cadiz we were not asked for passports, any more than we had been in Málaga and Valencia. On the other hand, when we entered Spain by the land frontier, and also later on leaving to go to Bayonne, we were asked for passports and a fee. It would appear that if one comes into Spain by sea, then one can journey throughout the country without a passport.

The Customs examination was very cursory and, after the usual extortion on the part of the boatmen and bearers, we ended up in the *Fonda de Paris*, in every way an excellent hotel.

Cadiz surprised me by its clealiness; there were many attractive whitewashed buildings and a lot of flag-staffs, but otherwise it had nothing special to offer the visitor. There was no picture gallery, no Moorish remains of any consequence and the streets, though crowded, did not have the colourful life that we had seen in Gibraltar. For us, coming as we did from the Moroccan coast, there was nothing novel here, nothing characteristic and striking, as there was over there. Cadiz did not really impress us. Perhaps it would have done so had we come there overland from the north. But there was one splendour here – the sea, the great rolling sea. The *Alameda* is well situated and offers a view out over the broad, open bay. Great waves broke over the sea-wall, sea-gulls flew screaming over the foaming billows; scores of fishing boats, looking like a flock of enormous birds, with great outspread wings, were making their way into harbour. Ships lay at anchor in the roads, flying the flags of all nations. In the *Alameda* there were long flower-beds, fenced in, and at each corner of the broad promenade there was a palm tree. There were a number of statues. The wind was cooler than over in Africa, although the sun was warm and it was still summer-like. All the same, Cadiz struck no chord in me – perhaps it was my fault, perhaps Cadiz itself was to blame. I looked at it from the *Alameda*, I looked at it from the harbour walls, from the market place and streets; I looked at it from my hotel window, from where I could see people on the flat roofs, hanging out their least mentionable garments to dry. . . .

Like all big towns in Spain, Cadiz has a very elegant casino, where one can find a lot of Spanish and foreign newspapers. We were very kindly introduced there.

When in 1835 people in Saragossa began to burn the monasteries and murder the monks, and the revolution spread from there over the whole country, Cadiz gave the monks there five hours' grace to vacate their monasteries. A watch was set outside to prevent arson; the mob seized all the provisions inside and burnt the chattels and books, but the buildings were left. Cadiz has no ruins to show from this time, there are no traces of any trouble; one has the impression that order and cleanliness are paramount here, that one is in a big trading centre, where romance can be found only in the view over the sea – and in Andalusian eyes. . . .

The countryside here does not invite one to make excursions. Jerez de la Frontera, which is not far away, was the only place said to be worth seeing – and that not to see churches or historical monuments but indeed to admire the great stores of wine and to wonder at this kind of splendour.

There is not much to recount from Cadiz : it was a poor beginning to our journey home from Tangier. Spain had not yet given me the material for a single story and it began to look as if I should not be able to fulfil my promise to the children at home, who were expecting a really Spanish story.[1]

Wandering through the town, I passed an open workshop where a young cabinet-maker was working at his bench. He was singing cheerfully and it was a German song. I stopped and spoke to him therefore in his mother-tongue and he became even more cheerful. He looked very Nordic, blonde with red cheeks and blue eyes; he came from a little place in Würtemberg and was shortly to be married in Cadiz. He radiated happiness and joy – as he stood and polished a coffin. But if one thinks about it, there is nothing sad in this. In the summer a beautiful tree grows in the wood; the sun shines, the birds sing and the wind rocks the green branches. The tree is cut down, that is its destiny. It is sawn into four good planks, which are brought to the joiner's workshop.

There is food for thought here. Four boards, with a little velvet and gold which soon decay, are a king's last kingdom; four boards await us all, rich and poor alike. . . .² Meanwhile the young joiner worked away at a coffin – and thought of his bridal bed. This was the only interesting encounter I had in Cadiz.

I am sure that a few days with the herdsmen on the vast plains of the Guadalquivir would have given me richer material. The river winds broadly up to Seville and is navigable for big ships all the way. Before the railway was established most of the traffic went by water. I have no doubt that a trip with a communicative smuggler would have provided material for a whole book. It is not so many years ago that more than one young man in Anda-lusia found himself playing a leading part in one or other of the guerrilla skirmishes during the civil wars. His first performance, the test of his courage and bravery, would certainly have been in a robbery or a little ambush; but this would not have seemed to him to be dishonourable. Perhaps, in the street or at the harbour, I stood by the side of such a person, a fitting hero for a very interesting story. I am sure Cadiz conceals material for a novel but the stranger does not see it.

We were advised to take the train up to Seville and not to try the tedious journey by steamer. We took the afternoon train. For the first few miles the train goes along the coast, where big waves were rolling in. The countryside was uncommonly flat; the sand had drifted inland for a long way, right up to the vast salt flats.

It was very desolate and barren. Pyramids of salt, such as we had seen in France round Cette, rose up from the grey-brown earth. We stopped at a couple of stations by the sea and then the landscape began more and more to take on the character of heathland. Dwarf palms were the most common shrub here; a great pinewood, the biggest we had yet seen in Spain, stretched up over the hills. The sun went down, the sky took on its evening glory – one looked into endless golden space. We approached Jerez de la Frontera, which has a special interest for historians. As is well known, it was here in the year 711 that the young General Tariq, only twenty years old, fought for nine days without ceasing and won a victory which, consolidated under the Viceroy of Ceuta, brought the whole of Spain under the Ommayad Caliphate.

We halted at a railway station a long way from the town; we could see its churches and whitewashed houses outlined in the clear evening air, but soon, as we went on again, they were hidden behind heath-covered hills. It got darker and darker; here and there a bonfire flared up close by the railway line and as we went by we caught a glimpse of people sitting around the fires.

We flew towards Seville, Murillo's birthplace, where Cervantes wrote part of *Don Quixote*, the city to which belongs the story of Don Juan, where he died, a pious holy man and where is his grave with the epitaph he wrote himself. The train hurried on, puffing and panting. It was dark all round now, so that we could not see the many towers of the town, the splendid *Giralda* or the ancient walls from Julius Caesar's time. We could only see the smoke of the train, which floated away like the misty spirits from the burial of Don Juan – but it was not yet the witching hour.

At eight o'clock in the evening we reached Seville, where we got out. The train went on to Córdoba, where the line ends.

XIII

Seville

We stayed in Seville at the *Fonda de Londres*. My balcony looked out on to the *Plaza Nueva*, which is very broad and planted with avenues of fruit-laden orange trees. A lot of marble benches were provided for weary walkers. The air was clear, with countless stars. I sat out on my balcony and enjoyed a cigar.

The cathedral in Seville, which is the largest church in Spain, the Moorish *Alcázar* and, last but not least, the matchless paintings of Murillo, make Seville one of the most interesting cities in Europe. It is rich in song and legend, in memories of the past and great names; the whole city has been set to music and painted in melody, for example in Rossini's *Barber of Seville*.[1]

The cathedral was once a mosque, but the architect has shown great talent in converting and adding to the original building. The cupola seems to sway, borne up by some unseen power; the great hall has been extended and heightened and is now a most magnificent church, with chapels and other additions, each one a church in itself. The wood carvings, the beautiful pictures in the great glass windows, the majesty and splendour of the whole style of the building, overwhelm and transport us. The walls are rich with paintings by Murillo, among them one of his most famous, 'Saint Anthony'. Outside the church there is the slender Moorish bell-tower, *La Giralda*, the highest in Spain. Twenty-five bells swing round up there; on the topmost point, shining in the sunlight, is a winged female figure representing Faith. One can ride a horse right to the top of the tower, so even and gently sloping is the ascent.

In front of the west entrance to the cathedral is the old Moorish *Patio de los Naranjos*, a courtyard planted with orange trees, where water ripples and splashes. A pulpit of hewn stone has been erected out here in the open air. Before the east entrance lies the exchange, *Lonja*, a vast, square building, in the court of which there is a small statue of Christopher Columbus. A broad stone staircase leads up to big rooms adorned with handsome cabinets in which are preserved the archives, documents relating to America from its discovery to the present day.

From *Lonja* one comes to the palace of the Moorish kings, the beautiful *Alcázar*. It is so well-preserved, the gold and colours are so fresh, that it looks as if it belonged to a period near our own time, as if it were only a few weeks since the Moors went away. Granada's *Alhambra* is like a vision seen in a dream, conjured up in the wonderful, clear moonshine of the south. The *Alcázar* in Seville is no vision, it is a reality; one can believe that the mighty princes and their lovely ladies could suddenly appear. Everything in the *Alcázar* is so fresh, so alive, our eyes are astonished by the wealth of colours and gilding. Here is the wonderful porcelain decoration, like lace, that one saw in the *Alhambra*; the doors are a coloured mosaic of inlaid wood. One stands, as it were, in a magic building where the walls are made of kaleidoscope pictures and Brussels lace, on what seems to be a gold ground, the whole borne up on slender, light, marble pillars. Although the eye cannot follow all the details of the arabesques, it rests with pleasure on the way the branching scrolls seem to flower into the arabic inscriptions. A higher storey was added later to accommodate the Spanish kings when they wanted to stay in Seville; it somewhat detracts from the building's original beauty, but this is still paramount. The inner court, the centre hall of the palace it might be called, the high hall where God's heaven is the ceiling, has something so magical about it that one might be in a fairy castle. The *Alcázar* belongs to the Arabian Nights, one is completely overwhelmed by Eastern beauty and splendour. Everything is in the same style and yet so varied. We should scarcely be surprised if Harun al Rashid and the Princess Sheherazade were suddenly to walk by.

We walked out into the garden, which is surrounded by buildings reminiscent of the Renaissance period, heavy but characteristic, blending however with the old-fashioned way in which the garden is laid out. Stiff myrtle hedges had been clipped and low, broad beds of flowers planted in the shape of arms, crowns and maps; even the orange trees had not been allowed to retain their lovely natural forms – the shears had trimmed them too into different shapes. In the middle of stone dams, grottoes and a rock garden had been made. Stone-paved paths cross each other and could be put under water – at the press of a button hundreds of jets of water sprang from a series of holes in these paths, cooling the hot air. In the centre of the garden is a little Moorish pavilion, which looks like an artificial flower made of limestone and moss, a curious rococo construction both inside and out.

Here in the *Alcázar* garden it was still summer and blessedly warm; the oranges hung full and thick among the dark leaves and there was a wonderful scent of roses. Underneath the building are the Moorish baths; we saw a walled basin, broad as a carriage-way and long as a dance hall. Once this was filled with clear water and the Sultanas bathed here; now one can walk through it. We were shown a door in the walls, now bricked up, through which the Moorish king would visit his harem.

In the streets of the town I found the air a little chilly and one had to walk on the sunny side to feel summer-like. In the shade, both morning and evening, there was a coolish autumn air – but then we were, after all, in November. The days, however, were warm and the air not at all oppressive. At home in the north we would have described it as lovely weather, were it even half as good as here.

Seville is the birthplace of Murillo and it was here that he mostly lived and worked. The walls of the Academy of Art are adorned with twenty-four of his unforgettable pictures. The well-known English painter, John Phillip, and the Swedish artist, Lundgren,[2] whose acquaintance we had made, took us to the gallery. The Murillo room was opened up and for the first time I realized the greatness of this artist. No one surpasses him : each one of these pictures is a joy to behold, but for me the most moving of all and the picture to which I returned again and again was that of 'Saint Anthony'. He is portrayed as a young man, the down just showing on his cheeks; the Holy Scriptures lie before him and in the middle of the Book sits the Infant Jesus, happy and smiling. Saint Anthony is bending towards the Child : his hands dare not touch Him, but his face shines with inner joy and veneration that is a benediction to behold.

There is one more of Murillo's pictures that I would include in the memorable things I saw in Seville, namely his 'Moses in the Wilderness'. This is in the church *La Caridad*, which is attached to the Hospital for aged and infirm men, founded by Don Juan Tenorio.[3] The picture is beautifully composed, full of life and movement. Water gushes forth and one child is stooping down to drink, while another child, somewhat bigger, politely waits to use the same bowl. There is a matchless truth and beauty in these two children. An attractive boy is sitting on a mule – I shall never forget his living face! Murillo is unsurpassed in painting children, so true to nature.

In the corner of this church hangs a remarkable work by Valdes, Murillo's teacher. It represents 'Annihilation'. One sees an Archbishop in his coffin; his Bishop's crozier is broken in pieces – it is only a rotting piece of wood – and the body of the dead man is in decay. This is portrayed so vividly that it is horrible and it is said that every time he passed this picture Murillo held his nose, so faithfully is the corruption reproduced.

After the monks were expelled from the monastery of *La Caridad*, the hospital was much enlarged and pious sisters now nurse the sick. The founder, Don Juan Tenorio, who died as a monk in this monastery, rests here; he himself wrote his epitaph : 'Here lies the worst man in the world.'

The story goes that Don Juan Tenorio was a young, pleasure-loving aristocrat in Seville, proud, witty and sensual in the extreme. He seduced the daughter of the Commandant, killed the father and sank in his ungodliness into the abyss. Another Spanish tradition calls him Don Juan de Mañara, one of Spain's richest noblemen, who led a wild life of pleasure, spending his nights in bacchanalian orgies. In his unbridled arrogance he even bade *La Giralda* step down from her tower and visit him one night; she moved her heavy copper wings which cut through the air and she came to him with heavy steps, such as later were given to the

Commandant's marble statue. But one midnight, when he was returning home through the silent deserted streets, he suddenly heard music, long wailing tones; he saw the flicker of torches and a great funeral procession approached. The corpse lay decked out in silver and silk on an open bier. 'Who shall be buried this night?' he asked and the answer came, 'Don Juan de Mañara!' The winding-sheet was lifted aside and Don Juan saw himself, lying there dead, stretched out on the bier. Mortal fear seized him and he fell senseless to the ground. The next day he gave all his fortune to the monastery, *La Caridad*, and himself entered the Order and was thereafter spoken of as one of the most penitent and pious of the Brothers.

The names Tenorio and Mañara in these two legends certainly refer to one and the same person. The Spanish writer, Tirso de Molina, was the first to dramatize this story, calling it *The Seducer of Seville and the Stone Guest.* (*El Burlador de Sevilla y Convidado de Piedra*): the name Don Juan Tenorio was retained although the family were still living at that time. Many versions of the play were produced in France and Italy, but Molière was the first to bring it to perfection. Later it was rewritten as the libretto for Mozart's opera which, with its immortal music, will carry the Don Juan story from generation to generation. Already in Tirso's version there is the whole of the dramatic ending as we know it. The marble statue of the Commandant comes from the grave; it knocks but the servant dares not open the door. Don Juan seizes a silver candlestick and goes himself to meet and light the way for his stone guest, who with marble-heavy steps enters the dining-room. The dead man is entertained with ices, cheerful songs and flippant questions about the other world. When he leaves he invites Don Juan to visit him in the mortuary chapel the following night. At the appointed hour Don Juan arrives with his terrified servant; a satanic meal has been prepared, 'scorpions and snakes and the wine is the bitterest gall.' The grasp of the cold, stone hand draws the seducer into the flames of the abyss. Don Juan sinks into the earth with the dead man, as the terrified servant crawls on his hands and knees to the front of the stage. . . .

In the church of *La Caridad* where Don Juan Tenorio once joined in pious chants with the other monks and prayed for his heavily burdened soul, his picture can be seen hanging on the wall. Every feature speaks of suffering and sorrow. There is a red cross on his black robe. Beneath his portrait hangs the sword with which he killed the Commandant, Don Gonzalo.

From *La Caridad* with its memorials and pictures we went to the *Casa de Pilatos* which, without doubt, must be reckoned as one of the glories of Seville. This house was built in the Middle Ages by order of the Duke of Alcala and is supposed to be an exact reproduction of the Roman Governor's house in Jerusalem. Every historical feature has been copied, even to the marble pillar in the courtyard where the Saviour was bound and scourged. The whole building with all its wealth and marble and porcelain is very reminiscent of the *Alcázar*. In each corner of the large forecourt there are antique marble statues, but for the rest, the garden has more a feeling of solitude and desolation than of the romantic charm which pervades the small Moorish gardens of Málaga.

One more building must be mentioned, the tobacco factory, which is almost like a whole town in itself. It sends cigars out to the whole of smoking Spain – and here one smokes in the theatre foyer and all the corridors; tobacco smoke even penetrates into the boxes. From the Seville factory snuff pours out over the whole peninsula; five hundred workers, mostly women, are employed in this vast tobacco-box. I did not visit it myself and therefore feel under a greater obligation to recommend it to other visitors.[4]

'Who has not seen Seville, has seen no wonders!' is a Spanish saying and there is always a nub of truth in folk proverbs and sayings. If Seville lay where Cadiz lies, by the rolling open sea, it would be a Spanish Venice and, what is more, a living Venice, a wonder of the first order, full of poetry and beauty, excelling other cities of the world, whatever they have to offer in the way of shops and palaces, broad streets and all else that good city authorities can bring about.

In Paris one tires oneself out looking at shops which can be amusing enough : one goes as in a treadmill, looking and looking and time passes and one gets home weary – and has profited nothing. It is quite otherwise in Seville. The streets are narrow and one is not dazzled by shops. The houses and courtyards look very ordinary, rather tediously over-whitewashed – but it is very much the same with them as it is with human beings: outside one looks very like another, but inside, there lies the difference and it is this that one comes to love more than the outward appearance. Walk through the streets of Seville and look inside; the doors and gates are open. *El patio*, as the little courtyard is called, is both the heart and the face which reveals to us the taste of the inhabitants. In one court there is a lovely statue, in another a big, carved, stone wall; the next house has perhaps a Moorish hall with stucco-work and artistic decoration. Let us cross the street where there lies a palatial building: its court is a whole rose-garden with fountains and statuettes. The little house close by has only a low small door into a tiny courtyard, but it is filled with lovely flowers around a single, tall palm. Now we are standing before a larger building with a colonnaded courtyard, three storeys high, decorated with oil paintings. Such is the variety of Seville. In late November there was not the outside life that goes on at other times. One should come to Seville in the spring when the flowers are at their best, or in the summer when one can see how the southerner lives. Then each little *patio* presents a conversation piece. The inhabitants spend their whole day down there, a big sun-awning is spread high over the courtyard or a vine forms a thick roof with its broad, shade-giving leaves. The family and servants sit there in the shade, working, gossiping or just dreaming lazily. During the long, warm days they stay out in the open air and go inside only at night to sleep.

People who live in the south need coolness and shade and Seville has plenty of both. The *Alameda* along the river Guadalquivir is most frequented. Poplars and plane trees provide shade, and waterfalls and fountains cool the air between the flowering hedges. The crowd moves along by carriage, on foot and on horseback, looking at each other and at the many ships behind the breakwater, some of which have come in from the Atlantic, others from the Mediterranean. Out towards the river is the octagonal *La Torro del Oro* where once the Moorish kings kept their treasure and from where, according to tradition, there is a secret underground passage to the *Alcázar*. A fine bridge leads over the river to the Triana district where many gypsies are to be found. Out there too lay the old, terror-inspiring prisons of the Inquisition, which are now, so I was told, used as store-houses for wines and spirits. Orange groves surround the shining white houses. I walked out that way. There was a crackle of castanets and some young women were dancing, most gracefully but with all the fire of youth.

In Seville, as in Málaga, one can pay to see folk-dances given by the Corps de Ballet. It was not my fate to see Spanish dancing in the theatre in Spain, but I did see something of it on country roads, in gardens and in the halls where the 'ballerinas' were giving special folk-dance performances.

There is all the difference in the world between French and Spanish dancing. If Paris represents France, then the cancan is the dance most characteristic of Paris and therefore of France. It is so free, so wanton, that one is reminded of the dance of the Bacchantes, but the Bacchantes were classic beauties with their flowing hair. The grisettes, those cancan virtuosos, are dressed for the street, with long skirts which must be lifted up so that they can use their limbs and begin the wild movements which, as they jump and kick, typify the whole of Parisian life, its restlessness and rush. She who can swing her leg highest over her cavalier's head is the best cancan dancer. The Spanish dance, on the other hand, allows the beauty of the human form to be seen in natural movement : the castanets blend in unison with the beating of the pulse – the blood may quicken but the dance is always beautiful. The Graces might observe it when they would flee from the Maenads. Venus herself might dance the Spanish dance, but she would never dance the cancan were Mars himself to invite her !

Seville has at least two large theatres. We visited the *Teatro de San Fernando*, which is light and friendly inside, with four tiers of seats and high boxes in the pit. Two performances are given daily, one beginning at three o'clock in the afternoon, the other at eight o'clock in the evening. I saw the latter when they were giving a two-act *zarzuela* called *Llamada y Tropa*. The word *zarzuela* means a sort of vaudeville: in practice it is more what we would call an operetta, although it often includes grand arias which really belong to opera. This one had music by the Spanish composer Arrieta, who seemed to be very prolific: most Spanish operas bear his name. The music was lively and had a rather French tone. Castanets and folk-songs were included and the dialogue was in verse. The local feature of the performance was the appearance of thirty *Niños del Asilo*, that is to say, charity children, the real orphans of Seville, who came on stage and sang a comic chorus. They acquitted themselves well and the public threw bonbons to them, which the children eagerly scrambled to collect. The audience cried '*da capo*', the song was repeated and a new shower of bonbons followed. This rather destroyed the dramatic illusion but it was very amusing.

The 19 November was the reigning Queen Isabella's name-day, which was celebrated by the Seville authorities. Military bands played in the streets, the balcony of the town hall was covered with gold-fringed, coloured tapestries, above which hung a portrait of the Queen in a gilt frame. Two soldiers, real living people, stood at arms, under orders to stand there motionless like wooden soldiers, for more than an hour. I had already seen this kind of portrait-tableau at the festivities in Granada and here the same exhibition of torture was repeated. The sun shone straight into the faces of the two wretched men, who dared not move a muscle nor scarcely blink an eye. This was a ceremonial tradition and so far as this sort of thing is concerned Spain is still living in the past. . . .

Before we left Seville I had to see the *Alcázar* once more, and the unforgettable cathedral, which in its majesty makes an even deeper impression than St Peter's, Rome. The train left at four o'clock in the afternoon. The sun was shining, summer-like, on the youthfully gay city. . . .

XIV

Córdoba

When the journey from Seville to Córdoba could only be done by diligence or by horse, the route went past sun-scorched Ecija by the river Genil. The description of this town, as given by the latest travel-writer on Spain, Théophile Gautier, makes it sound as if it were in China or Japan, so that one would much like to go there, but we did not manage it. The railway follows a direct route, crossing the old road with which it will have nothing to do; it never had a very good reputation anyway and most of the stories of robberies we have heard from our fellow-countrymen happened on that road. It was there, some years ago, that the architect Professor Meldahl was robbed. The bandits took his sketch-book from him. 'Please let me have it back,' he said, 'it is no use to you, but of great value to me,' and the robber who had taken it did not disavow Spanish courtesy, but returned the book to him.

The train steamed away into the evening darkness; here and there we saw a bonfire blazing by a solitary hut near the railway line, with men, women and children sitting beside it who grinned and waved to us. Perhaps they were telling of how much better it was a few years ago when the slow, heavy diligence crawled along the lonely road and men of spirit could with ease make a good living : the horses were halted, pistols pointed, knives flashed and a brave man possessed himself of gold and property. Now those good old days were over !

It was nine o'clock at night before we reached Córdoba, the birthplace of Seneca. All the travellers who were going into the town were packed, every single one of them, into the only omnibus which was waiting at the station. How we managed to get in the good Lord and the driver alone know ! The luggage,

147

an incredible collection of goods, was piled on top : the carriage creaked and groaned beneath its load. The passengers were put inside, one in the lap of another : nearly everyone had packages, umbrellas or some sort of parcel and we were stowed away as if we were in a press. There was no lantern on the carriage or light on the road, which was just as nature had made it. The street we came into was so narrow that there was no room for people to stand or walk when the omnibus drove through and finally it became so narrow that we could not drive further. The omnibus stopped and we were squeezed through the door like an artist squeezing paints out of a tube : that is how it felt.

The street ended in a narrow alley between tall houses. The coachman pointed, saying that we should go that way up to the *Fonda Rizzi*, the town's best hotel. We stumbled towards the light of a lantern that shone at the end of the alley-way. When we got there the entrance was brightly lit and inside we saw, as in Seville, a handsome big courtyard, surrounded by arcades on marble columns and with roses and geraniums in flower and a splashing fountain. The stairways were decorative and covered with rush matting. Our rooms were high and airy but without heating and it was cold, bitterly cold. A *brasero*, a brasier of glowing coals, was brought up to warm the rooms while we were down in the dining-room. There were a lot of people there who were leaving that night for Madrid by diligence. They were an extraordinary collection of cripples and decrepit old people – one coughed, another limped, a third groaned and a fourth squinted. They could have served as models for the artist wishing to paint the Parable of the Kingdom of Heaven, about the king who sent his army to destroy the invited guests who would not come to his son's wedding and, when the wedding feast was ready, sent his servants out into the highways and byways to invite all they found there, and they came, both bad and good. There were subjects here for a painter with humour.

'Such people should stay at home and not travel!' said the waiter to us when the hospital inmates had departed and we were able to sit down at table.

Under Moorish rule, Córdoba was the capital, with a million

inhabitants, six hundred mosques and a hundred public baths. Art and science flourished here, and now – how different! One finds poor, narrow, empty streets; Córdoba has sunk down and is now just an insignificant provincial town. In one or two small rooms I saw, hanging up, a few pieces of *Cordobán*, the famous Córdoba leather, and in the meat market there was a reminder of the ancient splendour where the walls of some of the booths were still covered with porcelain tiles from the time of the Moors. Through the deserted lanes with low, whitewashed houses, we came out on to the *Alameda* which, with its high old trees, follows the course of the Guadalquivir. The river was deep here, with a strong current : its waters were yellow as the Tiber. The life and traffic on the long, broad *Alameda* consisted of an old woman who, with great dignity, carried a large earthenware pitcher across the promenade and down the steep steps to the river, where three or four men sat on the remains of a wall out in the water, with fishing rods, waiting patiently for a bite. At the end of the *Alameda* are the ruins of an old monastery with its church. The walls were painted with religious pictures but were so cracked that they did not look able to bear the heavy stone images of the saints. We were told that during the persecution of the monks in 1835 this monastery had been stormed. The picture of disorder which the ruins now present brought vividly to mind all the bloody and dreadful scenes when the mob drove the monks back into the burning building and, in their fury, women kept the fires ablaze and prevented those inside from escaping.

From the *Alameda* there is a view over the broad, rushing river to the countryside, a fertile landscape with hills, olive groves and, here and there, a tall palm tree and the ruins of a great tower silhouetted on the horizon. Behind the town to the north are the mountains of the *Sierra Morena*, dark-blue and forbidding. The air was heavy with clouds. In Seville there had been no rain for five months; now it was beginning to fall in Córdoba and would soon probably visit Seville.

Córdoba does possess one treasure that is unrivalled by any other Spanish town, that is the great Mosque which is now the cathedral. It lies by the *Alameda*, out towards the river. It covers a vast area but the exterior is unremarkable, neither picturesque nor impressive. There is a large courtyard in front, planted with rows of orange trees by which run conduits of fresh, rippling water. The high bell-tower is separate from the church itself.

The mosque was built by King Abderrahman I : no less than one thousand and eighteen marble pillars bear up the arched roof – it looks like a whole forest of columns, planted in avenues, side by side and crossing each other. There are lower colonnades, innumerable pillars and arches and, along the four outer walls, altar after altar. It is always twilight in here, even on the brightest day. Through this forest half-light one comes to the centre point where, in Moorish times, thousands upon thousands of lamps always burned beneath the magnificent carved ceiling. Now this has gone and in its place there is a lofty, white-plastered, richly gilded Christian church, into which full daylight falls on a great shining altar, before which the censers swing as masses are sung, echoing through the Moorish arches where altars now stand, where chapels are raised in memory of those who have died in the Faith of salvation. One of my friends has graphically described the cathedral in Córdoba as being like a thick pine forest, in the centre of which a clearing has been made for a choir of tall beeches. In one of the side-chapels was a bed with a sick man: he was awaiting healing or release to God. The lace-like carving over the low door towards the river reminds one of the *Alcázar* and the *Alhambra*. During the rule of the Mussulmen holy relics were preserved here : there was a very ancient manuscript of the *Koran* and the right arm of the Prophet Mahomet. The pious among the faithful approach this place only on their knees; it is still the most interesting spot in the whole building and has retained its original beauty.

While from the choir hymns of praise are sung to Jesus and the Virgin Mary, arabic inscriptions on the walls proclaim, 'There is only one God and Mahomet is his Prophet.' The whole building makes a strange, jumbled impression, the best effect of which should be to make us tolerant for, in the words of the hymn, 'We believe, we all believe in God.' . . .[1]

From this thought-provoking, awe-inspiring sanctuary one

comes out by the river, over which there is a fine old Roman bridge. Out in the water one can see the remains of Moorish bridges and buildings; the yellow water streams through and over these dumb reminders of the past. . . . We made our way up through broken stones, where trees grew wild and hedges spread themselves like a veil of forgetfulness over vanished glory and splendour. Here was the beautiful *Alcázar* of the Moorish kings, with its carved marble arches, its rose gardens and fountains. Here echoed music and song, here resounded the drums and trumpets in days and nights of festivity. But all this splendour vanished like clouds away, and darkness and anguish followed. The Spanish Inquisition moved into these halls, walled up the light, airy casements and set up instruments of torture where once soft cushions were spread; the anguished screams of the victims being tortured to death were heard where once the lute was played and gentle voices echoed. The cannon-balls of the French soldiers battered down these walls; in the garden the wild-growing hedges and ancient trees were bruised and burnt; broken stones and rubbish were all that was left of past glory. . . .

Was it by chance or is it characteristic of Córdoba, the city of song, where under the Moors a whole school of music was founded, that now no song was to be heard, no sound of castanets, and no dancing was to be seen. It seemed to be desolate and deserted; a solitary Señora, prayer book in hand, hurried through the narrow streets to the ancient cathedral, Córdoba's glory and pride.

On the outskirts of the town there is a little church, also once a mosque and now consecrated to Saint Nicholas. The tower is remarkable – it is, quite unchanged, the old minaret, probably the only one now remaining in Spain. In front is a small square planted with trees, from which there is a lovely view over to the dark range of the *Sierra Morena*, once the terror of travellers, for here roved the most notorious, bloodthirsty robber-bands. The highway from Córdoba to Madrid goes that way, through La Mancha, Don Quixote's land, and into Castilla La Nueva.

While I stood here in the little square and enjoyed the view of that impressive landscape, the heavy rainclouds began to

disperse and the rays of the sun pierced through, falling, sharply
defined, on to the brownish-green *campaña*. The mountains became dark as night; an armed peasant on his mule was the only
living object to be seen in this vast solitude.

9 Copy by John Phillip of detail of *Las Meninas* by Velasquez. The original is in the Prado, Madrid.

10 The cathedral at Burgos.

11 Toledo, with the Alcazar and the River Tagus.

XV

Through Santa Cruz de Mudela to Madrid

The largest stretch of the railway line from Córdoba to Madrid is not yet completed, one has to take the diligence. It is drawn by ten mules and, fast as it goes, whatever the state of the road, one still has to endure about twenty-three hours in this vehicle before reaching Santa Cruz de Mudela, where the railway to Madrid starts. We booked seats in the diligence for as far as it went and intended to stay and rest in Santa Cruz.

The street in Córdoba where the diligence office was situated is so narrow that it is impassable for vehicles; we had therefore to walk to the nearest broader street where the diligence was waiting. There were only three passengers so there was plenty of room. The vehicle was not bad and neither was the weather; the sun came out, the *mayoral* cracked his whip and shouted his *'Thiah! Caballo de desbocada, Gitana, Golondrina'* and other meaningful names. We drove through the main street, along the *Alameda*, out through the old city gate. The *campaña* lay before us, smiling and rich in olive trees, but very sparsely inhabited. The sun had not yet gone down when we reached Andujar, a town which, with its shops and crowded streets, looked quite different from Córdoba which is much bigger. Here we were joined by a really cheerful travelling companion, not young but as susceptible as though he were in the bloom of youth. To every woman he saw, whatever her age, he threw a kiss and cried, 'You are the light of my life, your eyes are as two suns!' He exerted himself so much doing this that he was obviously very tired when, in the evening, we reached Bailen, a fairly considerable place, famous in the history of the wars. We stopped on the outskirts of the town to change mules. It was a still, lovely evening, with a new moon which looked like a golden bowl in which lay a dark-blue

F   153

ball. We had stopped by the entrance to a churchyard; two priests in long, black cassocks were walking like ghosts under the dark trees. The moon shone on the windows of the church, which glittered as though they were lit from within. The river Guadalquivir rushed along close by : we could hear the stream, the only sound, monotonous and sleep-inducing, in the vast solitude. . . .

Our susceptible Spaniard said he would dream of beautiful eyes – and shut his own. I gazed out into the clear night and dozed a little, but there is not much to say about a journey by diligence at night. One remembers a glimpse of countryside lit by the moon or a stable lantern, the outline of a shadowy figure. From this journey I remember only that we drove through flat, cultivated land and that, long before daybreak, we reached the little town of La Carolina, peacefully sleeping. It was a German colony, but the German language had died out there many years ago.

The carriage door was flung open by a very stout woman, holding up a lantern which lit up her own face. She cleared her throat and opened her mouth to speak, but no words came : instead she sneezed and our amorous Spaniard wished her the blessing of heaven and a handsome sweetheart.

Inside the inn, the first thing they set before us was a large and very welcome *brasero* full of glowing coals, to warm us poor frozen mortals; then we were given hot chocolate and so came sufficiently back to life to be stuffed into the carriage again, where now all the places were occupied. It was a difficult, uncomfortable drive. From La Carolina the road went continually uphill, between jutting-out rocks; we looked down into deep ravines, still misty in the morning twilight. The countryside became more and more wild and picturesque. The *Sierra Morena* mountains rose before us in all their grandeur and variety. It was really beautiful! Gigantic fallen rocks lay as though thrown down from the hills; great trees twined their long roots fast round the stones, bending their heads down over ravines where, in the depths below, waters roared and dashed on their way. We met two armed soldiers who, for our safety, escorted us part of the way. I do not think we were really in danger of ambush, indeed

I felt so safe that I suddenly had a tremendous desire to experience just a little encounter with bandits. The whole area seemed designed for this and I can well understand, if it were true – which it is not – that Alexander Dumas, when he was travelling in Spain, absolutely insisted on being ambushed, as much for his own enjoyment as for that of his readers. Spaniards have told me this story to illustrate how safe travel is now. Before he went to Spain, Alexander Dumas is said to have sent a well-known robber chief a draft for a thousand francs, asking him, in return, to arrange an attack on his party without, of course, any loss of life or real danger. The robber wrote back that his firm had been closed down and the business was no longer carried on, but he acknowledged the cheque with thanks and sent a receipt. The whole story is, of course, made up.

In such country as this one should not ride in a diligence but rather in the old-fashioned way, on horseback; one should see these mountains not only in broad sunlight but also by the light of the moon. We walked for a long way but could scarcely keep warm : it was very cold and round about the water was covered with ice. At last the sun came out and we could see signs of life. Workmen were busy blasting rocks and tunnelling through hills where the railway between Córdoba and Madrid is to run – it should be finished in a couple of years. The workers lived in huts thatched with fresh, green cactus leaves and lying but a short distance apart from each other. The women sat outside, dressing their children, and some families were already eating their breakfast. There was matter enough for many sketches, were I to describe everything we saw and, in a few seconds, passed by.

About eleven o'clock in the morning we reached the little town of Santa Cruz de Mudela. I have not seen such a dirty place in the whole of Spain. The streets were unpaved and were at that moment covered with thick, evil-smelling mud. It was impossible to walk here, impossible to get a breath of fresh air. The houses were just wretched, poor hovels. But we were obliged to go through the town, for all its mud and filth. A little way outside the railway station was the *fonda* which had been recommended to us; indeed it was the only one in the place. It did not look inviting; it was a big, dirty inn, with low, dingy rooms, where they had strewn straw on the floor to keep the feet warm. The bedroom they showed us had no proper window : there was a large, square opening in the wall with a wooden lattice that could be shut. This was all and it was said to be the best room in the house. To have passed the night here and then to have spent the next morning in this hole, or to have wasted the time in this poverty-stricken, uninteresting neighbourhood would have been a punishment and penance : I would rather have fainted or died of over-fatigue in the railway carriage.

The decision made, we put it into action at once. The train was due to leave in a few minutes and would get to Madrid about midnight, after a ten-hour journey. We were most comfortably seated; it was more than refreshing to be travelling in a civilized conveyance, to have the feeling once more of being in the present day. We went at a flying speed. The countryside was flat and monotonous. At the old city of Alcázar de San Juan which, with a couple of other Spanish towns, claims to be the birthplace of Cervantes, we joined the Madrid-Valencia line. We had to wait an endless time for the main-line train which was not due until well after sunset. In the meantime we sat in the very dull station and looked out over the old city, with its many churches and large buildings. They looked very interesting : we could have spent the night here and perhaps have made an excursion to nearby Toboso, famous through Don Quixote's Dulcinea, but no one had mentioned this place to us; we had been told that only in Santa Cruz de Mudela was there a *fonda* for travellers. Railways are such a novelty still in Spain, that even in the bigger towns one can get no information if they are not on the line. The printed railway guide, *Indicator de los Caminos de Hierro*, in which full and precise details are given of all the stations and trains, is not available in any station before one gets to Madrid.

Alcázar de San Juan stood, silhouetted against the red evening sky, when we steamed off again. It was a long journey and took a long time. The new moon stood in the heavens and showed us wide open countryside on both sides. Conversation in the carriage languished : it was confined to counting the hours and minutes we still had to pass before we reached the end of our journey. It was dark and became darker still when suddenly we came to Aranjuez, set among bushes and trees, an oasis in the desert of Madrid. Of course we at once thought of Schiller's verse in *Don Carlos*:

> *Die Schönen Tage von Aranjuez,*
> *Sind nun zu Ende.*[1]

We stopped a few minutes in the station, saw the street lamps shining in the avenues and reflected in the canals – and the minutes in Aranjuez were at an end. The train was on its way to Madrid and we should be there in an hour.

It was a long, dark hour: not a light from a house or *venta* twinkled at us. We were travelling over barren countryside which had once been woodland. As regards the name Madrid, the story goes that a little boy was pursued here by a bear: he clambered up a tree and shouted to his mother, who was coming to his aid, '*Madre, Id!*' – that is to say, 'Mother! Run!' Now we were running at full speed and looked out of the train to see if we could catch a glimpse of the city by lamplight. At one moment there were lights shining in the distance – it was Madrid – but then it vanished as the train rounded a bend.

At last we drew into the station; it was midnight. We were not subject to tiresome customs examination and were soon driving across the broad avenues of the *Prado* into the city. Through a couple of long streets we came to the *Fonda Peninsular*, the hotel recommended to us by everyone. At midnight, in a dim light, it looked very deserted and so dirty and dingy – with not a living soul to be seen anywhere – that we turned round and asked the cab-driver to take us to a better hotel. He recommended the *Fonda del Oriente*, not far away on the *Puerta del Sol*, said to be the best in the city. We drove there and were given excellent accommodation: a fire was blazing, good food and wine were set before us, the beds were good and I slept well and without dreams – and these are things to be remembered when one is sleeping for the first time in a strange place.

XVI

Madrid

The first day I had decided to stay in and rest. The weather was raw and unfriendly and much to my surprise all the roofs were covered with snow – winter had already come to Madrid. Down in the square below, where several of the principal streets of the city meet, it was dark and dirty. There were a lot of carriers' carts with mules, their bells jingling, droskies and other carriages on the move. I saw soldiers on horse and on foot, and peasants wrapped up in their great red *mantas* and with red basque bonnets on their heads. There were not many women about, the weather was too bad for them. The men slung their cloaks round them, right up over their mouths, but there was nothing particularly new or characteristic to be seen, although this was Madrid's most frequented *plaza*, the heart of the city, the *Puerta del Sol.* At first sight it was not very promising, but things might improve and perhaps we should find ourselves rooted fast in Madrid for the whole winter. A happy thought! Our Danish Minister, Baron Brockdorff, I knew to be a most amiable and kind man and I had already predicted to my companion that we would feel very much at home here in the capital of Spain. At the Legation we should also find letters from home; we had had none for a very long time and how much we longed for news!

The porter in the hotel said, 'There is no Danish Minister in Madrid, otherwise I would know where he lived.' A cab-driver was then asked: he thought about it for a long time, driving in his thoughts to all the Legations, but not a single country sounded like '*Dinamarca*'. He called a second cabby who consulted a third, and the throng of cab-drivers grew until finally they found a well-informed one – who drove us straight to the Belgian Minister's. Here we were told that there was no Danish Legation

in Madrid, but this just could not be true and we got the cab to
take us to the Foreign Ministry, where we were told that Baron
Brockdorff was in Denmark. This was sad news! All our long-
awaited letters, where were they? We went to the post office to
try to discover where letters addressed to the Danish Legation
were delivered and we were informed that in such-and-such a
street, in such-and-such a house and on such-and-such a floor
there lived a gentleman who was not attached to the Legation
but who, in the absence of the Minister, received all the letters
addressed to the same. Now we had only to find the house and,
when we had found it, hope to find the man at home. He turned
out to be a very obliging, kind Spaniard; the postman had
certainly brought him a letter addressed to me, but since he did
not know any Herr Andersen he had therefore let the postman
take the letter away again. The postman was not to be found and
the letter lay in his pocket. It was not very amusing. 'But', I
asked, 'for other matters, to whom can I now turn? Where will
our passports be stamped when we leave?' 'The Swedish Minister,
Excellency Bergman, will take care of that,' answered the Spaniard and promised to take us to him.

We got there in cold and rain and, as chance would have it,
he was not at home either. However, he was informed of our
arrival and already early the next day came a message and a
friendly greeting from the Swedish Minister. A few hours later
he himself walked into my room. We had known each other in
Naples: I was in the best of hands and with the kindest possible
person. He did everything he could for me and for my companion and we received daily proof of his care and attention.
With the best will in the world, the Danish Minister could not
have done more for us than did our Swedish friend and protector.
We were no longer alone and friendless. It turned out, however,
that all the letters I had brought to Madrid were useless: the
people to whom I had introductions were all away – the only one
I found at home was the writer, Don Sinibaldo de Mas, who had
been Spanish Minister in China, but he lay ill. I was doubly glad,
therefore, to have found a friend from 'hin sida sundet.'*

* The other side of the Sound, i.e. Sweden. G.T.

The weather was bitterly cold : during the day the snow indeed melted on the roofs, but the next morning they were white again. The air became clear with blue skies, but there blew a wind that I, who came from the Wind's home in the North, found diabolical : it was cold, piercing and dry. The Spaniards say, 'The wind in Madrid cannot blow out a candle, but it can well kill a man.'*

Madrid has none of the character of a Spanish city, let alone that of the capital of the country; that it is the capital was a whim of Philip II and he certainly must have frozen and sweated as a result of this, his royal will.

But there is of course one glory here, indeed the first of its kind, and that is the picture gallery. It is indeed a pearl, a treasure and alone worth making the visit to Madrid for. During our stay here there was one other great artistic enjoyment, the Italian Opera. Outside it was raw and damp, but inside the theatre one sat as in a bathroom, in smoke and steam : a thick fog of tobacco smoke from all the cigars that people smoked in the intervals, and the smell of gas pervaded all the boxes. All the same, one stayed there, one held out until after midnight, spellbound by the richness of the tones with which Signora La Grange refreshed and intoxicated us.[1]

The opera and the gallery – the latter a permanent pleasure – must, it may be argued, give Madrid an advantage over most other cities. But it is with places as with people, they either attract or repel. I would never choose Paris as my home; I have never felt comfortable in Venice – I have always had the feeling there that I was on a wreck at sea. Madrid reminds me of a camel that has fallen down in the desert – I was sitting on its hump, from which I had a good view, but I was not sitting comfortably and it was an expensive seat !

Besides the *Puerta del Sol*, where we were staying, there are in Madrid other *plazas* which one should mention, each with its

---

* '*El aire de Madrid es tan sotil*
 Que mata á un hombre
 Y no apaga á un candil.'
 H.C.A.

own special attraction. The most beautiful is the *Plaza de Oriente* by the royal palace. It is planted with trees and bushes and under the trees are groups of statues of the Kings and Queens of Leon and Castile. The palace itself is a big heavy building, but from its terrace and indeed from part of the *plaza* itself there is an extensive and lovely view over the garden and fields down to the river Manzanares, and over to the mountains behind the *Escorial*. They were now snow-capped and looked very picturesque when the air was clear and blue. The *Plaza Mayor*, which is not far from here, has a quite opposite character : here one feels as if one were confined in a prison-yard, but it is without doubt the most remarkable of all the *plazas* in Madrid. In appearance it is medieval, longer than it is broad, with a bronze statue in the middle of Philip III on horseback. The tall arcades all round offer only small, indifferent shops, selling caps, woollen scarves and hardware. In olden days this was the scene of bloody bullfights and the dreadful *autos-de-fé*. One can still see the old building, with its towers and carved windows, from the balcony of which the King of Spain and his court watched the bullfights and saw the wretched victims of the Inquisition burned alive. The little bell which gave the signal for death still hangs on the wall here. I always saw a lot of soldiers standing about in groups, watching one or other of the jugglers who throughout the day performed here. In the evening beggar boys had lit a fire to warm themselves and on the steps up to the arcade sat a couple of wretched-looking figures, an old woman in rags and a white-haired old man wrapped in a tattered, filthy cloak. Each of them was scraping away at a cracked instrument and singing in a voice equally cracked and hoarse. None of the passers-by gave them anything, but they went on all the same, sitting as if they had grown fast to the damp stone, in the raw, cold weather – and perhaps they were singing about that hero El Cid, or the pleasures of love.

The *Plaza de las Cortes* is small, really only an extension of the road in front of the National Assembly building, *Palacio de los Deputados*. The only point of interest for the foreigner is the monument which stands there, the statue of a man in old Spanish military dress, with a stiff ruff and sword. There is nothing grand about this memorial and one could easily pass it by, thinking it had been erected to commemorate some military hero who has no particular claim on our thoughts or hearts today. But when we hear the name we stop, filled with joy and thanksgiving, for his works are immortal, his memory blessed throughout the civilized world. While in vigorous manhood he bore the chains of a slave; for his fatherland, Spain, he gave his left arm in battle. His own generation let him suffer hunger and need, treating him with irresponsible indifference : they could neither comprehend nor appreciate him. Now his monument stands here with the inscription :

A Miguel de Cervantes Saavedra
Principe de los Ingenios Españoles

The author of *Don Quixote* and of *Galatea*, founder of the drama, teller of folk-tales,* was as remarkable a writer as a person. The many and heavy trials he went through did not embitter him but, on the contrary, seemed to act as a spur to his rich humour. Every true poet must see in him an example of human endurance and true modesty. Already in his lifetime his dramatic works were surpassed by the prolific and very witty Lope de Vega,† but he will never be surpassed as a novelist : *Don Quixote* will always be the novel above all novels. After this work, which he dedicated to Count Lemos, there followed *Persíles* and *Sigismunda*, a work of which he said himself, 'This will either be the worst or the best book written in our language.' 'The Journey to Parnassus' is his last poem, which adds to the lustre of his name with its light rhythms, with the colour and play

---

* Among his many short stories is the well-known '*La Gitanella de Madrid*'. H.C.A.
† Lope de Vega produced no less than 2,200 pieces for the theatre, as well as many long and short poems : one of these, *Angelica*, he wrote on board ship when doing military service in the so-called Invincible Armada which Spain sent against England. As a widower he entered holy orders and it is sad to have to add that the great writer took office with the Inquisition and even assisted at *autos-de-fé*. H.C.A.

of his wit and humour. His name rests on no gravestone, but in the hearts of the people. Spain is proud of this. Europe speaks of him with admiration and honours Cervantes.

The monument stands on the *plaza* in Madrid where the poet's house once stood.

With the memory of Cervantes, our thoughts fly over the whole rich field of Spanish literature and one is astonished by its fertility and national freshness which, in spite of all storms, shows itself even in our day. Before France, Spain had its Molière in the craftsman, the strolling player, Lope de Rueda.* We see, near to each other, the ever-green oaks of mighty genius, Cervantes, Lope de Vega, Calderon and Moreto.† The century in which they flourished seems to have been the highpoint for Spanish literature, although it has never afterwards been completely dead. Under all the bloody battles which this country has fought, even while the flames of torture and death blazed from the mouth of the dragon of the Inquisition, the national poetic spirit remained freshly alive.

We visited the museum, where the wealth of masterpieces to be found is overwhelming. Here are works by Raphael, Titian, Correggio, Paul Veronese and Rubens, but above all, Murillo and Velasquez. One would need to be in this place for more than a year and a day fully to absorb and appreciate all these riches. Here for the first time I saw and learned something about Velasquez,[2] who was a contemporary of Murillo. What art and genius he has shown in portraying the milk-white Infantas in the ridiculous costumes of the time. They are living, speaking and indeed can be regarded as beautiful by virtue of the perfection with which they are painted, and by comparison with the grotesque figures surrounding them – dwarfs, male and female, and ferocious-looking dogs of characteristic ugliness. The figures look so much as if they are about to walk out of their frames, that one cannot doubt the story that when a couple of these pictures were put up on easels in Velasquez' studio, folk in an

---

* His most active literary period was between the years 1544 and 1567.
† Moreto's celebrated comedy *Donna Diana* (*El Destén con el Desdén*) has been seen on the Danish stage. H.C.A.

adjoining room thought that the actual, living people were there. The King of Spain, Philip IV, was a friend and admirer of Velasquez, gave him the rank of Court Chamberlain and decorated him with the highest Spanish Orders.

There are no less than ten paintings here by Raphael, including one of his most famous, 'The Way of the Cross'. Next to it comes 'The Holy Family', the picture which Philip IV called 'the pearl', but this title is not deserved, either as a description of one of Raphael's works or indeed as indicating its place among the treasures to be found in this gallery.

But better than Raphael, better than Titian, better than all others for me, is Murillo. His Madonna, ascending to heaven surrounded by angels, is so perfect, so inspired, that one feels it must have been in a heavenly revelation that he saw and portrayed her. Another, smaller picture with a wonderful effect is that of the 'Infant Jesus', with a lamb and a shepherd's crook : in His face is an expression of assurance combined with child-like innocence. I must mention one more work by Murillo, beautifully felt and presented. It is a little domestic scene : the young mother sits, winding wool, the husband holds the child, a little bird is flying up in the air, while a little dog shows his tricks by sitting up and begging.

Outside Spain, Murillo is not known as he should be and therefore not given the high rank he merits above the other great artists.

The museum also owns some of Thorvaldsen's works : the sketch for his well-known bas-relief, 'The Guardian Angel', is found here and in it one can see a serpent by the child's foot which is not in the bas-relief.[3]

I had the opportunity of meeting a number of learned and literary persons in Madrid. Minister Bergman introduced me to the Duke de Rivas, one of Spain's most prominent figures in politics and literature. His popular work, *El Moro Exposito*, was widely acclaimed as, no less, was his tragedy, *Don Alvaro*. I was received very kindly by the old man, who remembered our previous meeting in Naples when he was Spanish Minister there. He talked about *Don Alvaro* which he had recently rewritten as a text for an opera by Verdi, who was in fact at that very time expected in Madrid to start on the music.[4]

I also got to know Don Juan Eugenio Hartzenbusch, another leading Spanish writer. *Los Amantes de Teruel*, written and produced in 1836, is his first original work : it was very well received. Several other excellent dramatic works followed, and his writings in prose and verse increased rapidly. Among these his *Cuentos y Fabulas* was particularly well received and is today known and loved wherever Spanish is read.

A letter to Hartzenbusch from one of our mutual friends in Málaga ensured me a very kind reception which, he said, I would have had without any letter of introduction. He spoke very warmly, and with appreciation, of me as a writer, although he can have known but few of my works. (So far as I was able to discover, only two of my stories have been translated, 'The Little Matchgirl' and *'Holger Danske'*. Not many people in Spain can read German and English, and the French translations are very bad : whole paragraphs have been rewritten, misunderstood or completely omitted.) Hartzenbusch was at that time working on a book about Cervantes and was also superintending a vast new edition of *Don Quixote*. Before we parted he gave me as a souvenir a copy of his *Cuentos y Fabulas*, in which he wrote a kind and cordial dedication.

The author, Don Sinibaldo de Mas, arranged a dinner party for me in one of the Madrid *fondas*. Among the writers I met there was Don Rafael Garcia y Santesteban, the author of *El Ramo de Ortigas* and several *zarzuelas*. They were all very friendly and full of enthusiasm, with all the Spanish courtesy and desire to be of service. One of my new young friends, Jacobo Zobel Zangroniz from Manila, was particularly tireless in this respect and sought in every possible way to make my stay in Madrid pleasant and comfortable.

I had thought at one time of staying in Madrid over Christmas and into the New Year, but although I had gradually made a lot of interesting acquaintances, had met with much kindness, had the opera and the art gallery to visit and each Sunday – if I wished – a bullfight, three weeks here was quite long enough, even though we were to use a few days of this visiting Toledo. The weather in Madrid was intolerable, with snow, rain and storm – it is never worse than this at this time of year home in Denmark – and if some days happened to be clear and dry, then the wind was so piercing, so sharp, that it got on one's nerves and one had the feeling of being mummified by it.

Our visit to Toledo was exhilarating and refreshing. We were once again in a genuine Spanish town, which has everything that Madrid lacks, including the features and character which the capital of the country should have. Ancient Toledo is medieval, picturesque and full of poetry.

XVII

Toledo

We left Madrid by the morning train and on the Valencia line reached Aranjuez, from where a branch line goes to Toledo. We were going over the broad *campaña* by daylight and it certainly looked better than it is reputed to do. It is not completely desert, much is already under cultivation and all of it will be in due course.

Near Aranjuez the landscape looked very Danish, with tall thick trees, a copse, a park, the whole intersected by canals enclosing some small lakes. We saw it in a cold, northern, autumn light.

The well-built little town, with its palace, open forecourt and park, seemed to be longing for people : it was friendly here but solitary and deserted, like a country place which the family have left. Under these old trees Philip II spent his 'happy days' : in the garden here Charles IV had his toys – a miniature fleet, with which he played happily.

The character of the countryside changes completely as soon as the train leaves Aranjuez for Toledo. I really thought we had suddenly moved to the country near Rome, the yellow Tagus is so like the Tiber.

We passed solitary farms and abandoned huts. Colourful groups of men and women were standing about at each stopping-place; lively, black-eyed girls waved down from balconies. On the whole of this stretch of line it looked as if the railway guards were mostly women : every few minutes we saw a mother, children holding fast to her skirts or sprawling around her, standing and waving a rolled-up flag in the direction the train was to go.

Towards midday we reached Toledo railway station and got

into an omnibus, which crawled up an even, good road between bare masses of rock, past a great ruin – and there before us, incredibly picturesque, was the ancient knightly city of Toledo. We drove over the dizzily high Alcántara bridge: deep down below, the yellow water rushed by, on its way driving a couple of water-mills which looked as if they had been thrown up by a flood and left on the bank. In the river lay ruins of several large buildings, with the strongly flowing stream forcing its way in where the lower windows had been, through the roofless rooms and out again. Ahead of us the town itself rose up from the ancient, yellowish-grey, ruined walls, towering up on the heights and crowned on the summit by the ruins of the *Alcázar*, the palace of Charles III.

On the other side of the Alcántara bridge, down under the city walls, the road swung round and we got a new view, which grew more and more picturesque as we continued to ascend. We could see old monasteries and ruined churches and all around the landscape was a sun-scorched, stony desert. The only sign of life was a flock of coal-black swine who were being driven down to the Tagus to drink or to wash – but we did not see which. The road turned again and we came on to a terrace with a stone balustrade, then in through the architecturally beautiful *Puerta del Sol.* We were now in Toledo. The road was narrow, the *Alameda* small and confined, with a few trees, stone benches and some very poor shops. Two soldiers and a street urchin were the only people about. The street was so steep that the omnibus soon stopped and could go no further. Our luggage was carried for us through a small alley-way, which went sharply down, with a dreadful, uneven surface and we reached the *fonda* which had been recommended to us.

Two donkeys stood in the hall and we were received by a couple of hens and a cock; a girl put her head round the door and then vanished. But then the Señora appeared and her kindly face lit up with pleasure when we gave her greetings from Jacobo Kornerup de Dinamarca.[1] Our fellow-countryman had lived here for a long time in this house and was much liked by the family.

We were given two cold bedrooms which connected with a

vast sitting-room into which the *brasero* was brought. It was so
cold that we could see our breath. The staff got busy : the oldest
hen was slaughtered, three large onions were peeled, the oil was
shaken in the pan and luncheon, the most wretched meal we had
had in Spain, was served. But it was also very cheap here and the
people were very kind. What was more important, Toledo is a
city in which there is something worth seeing.

We went straight up to the *Alcázar*. The Gothic King Wamba
was the first to build his castle here : it was later rebuilt and
extended by the Moorish and Castilian Kings. Charles III gave
it the magnificence which even today, in spite of destruction and
ruin, still astounds us. Vaulted cellars stretch under the palace
and the courtyard and they are so vast that several regiments
used them as stables simultaneously. The courtyard forms a
square, surrounded by arcades supported by heavy granite pillars.
The lower arcade is still standing but the storey above now has
only a single row of columns, bare walls with gaping stone casements and balconies jutting out without balustrades. Some goats
were leaping about up there and looked down at us with curiosity.
The heavy marble stairways looked as if they were about to
collapse. It was a picture of ruin and desolation. Only one wing
of the building is still habitable and soldiers are quartered there.
We saw them, some half-dressed, some in full dress with the red
trousers, brown jacket and the white *shako* of the uniform of the
Córdoba Regiment. Some of them were digging in the garden on
the terrace looking out to the Alcántara bridge.

The façade of the *Alcázar* is best preserved on that side. It is
still decorated on all storeys with statues and other embellishments, but this is only a thin shell, behind which the hand of
destruction has taken a heavy toll. From the terrace one looks
down over the tumble-down walls of the city to the river Tagus.
On the other side of the Alcántara bridge are the ruins of the old
citadel of San Servando.

Masses of bare, grey-green rock lie all around here, thrown
about in wild confusion as if the whole stony ground had been
forcibly blasted – no earthquake could have so shaken the fast
ground into pieces. There is a small path along the river bank,

which offers an ever-changing and picturesque view. One goes past solitary, brick water-mills; the path narrows into a track overhanging the yellow torrent, which forms one waterfall after another. The path mounts up again between the bare rocks, with not a tree, not a bush to be seen : it is as if one were walking in a deserted quarry – and suddenly the path itself seems to vanish and there is not a house, not a living soul in sight. One is in a stony desert. But on the other side of the river, Toledo proudly rises, a splendid ruin, with the *Alcázar* as its royal crown.

The walk from the Alcántara bridge to the San Martin bridge is unforgettable in its solitary, ruined grandeur. No birds sang or flew past us and only when we got near to the San Martin bridge did we see people – a couple of armed peasants on their mules, riding slowly down towards the open highway, which at one moment shrank into a mountain track scarcely broad enough for any vehicle.

Through the dingy city gate by the San Martin bridge one returns to the town. Roads and paths cross each other, leading up over great piles of rubbish and bits of buildings, to the church of *San Juan de los Reyes*. Its red walls are hung with heavy, iron chains which were struck from the Christian prisoners when the Moors were driven out. Inside the church there are many historic memorials. High up under the vaulted arches, supported by stone pillars, is the gallery from which Isabella and Ferdinand, the Catholic Kings, heard mass. Under it there is a remarkable, carved wooden figure of the Prophet Elijah. The folds of his clothes are soft and of fine workmanship. The Prophet's face is wonderfully alive. A candle was held up to the mouth and we could see the teeth and tongue, minutely and beautifully carved.

Next to the church are cloisters, which can really be called a garden : the place was full of oranges and rose bushes in flower, but no fountains played and the basins stood half filled with dry earth and withered leaves. All round were scattered the broken pieces of decorative tiles and other ornamentation. One could scarcely walk in the open colonnades, so littered were they with bits of masonry, altar-pictures and torsos of statues of the saints.

Spiders' webs hung like veils of mourning over these venerable remains.

The same decay and destruction is apparent in the streets nearby : for some long way there is neither gateway nor door to be seen, but here and there, high up, is a window, well-barred but empty like a deserted prison. There were no people about. A small alley with greyish walls went up higher and higher between piles of rubbish and dark, isolated houses. By a small, low door in a crumbling wall stood a little old woman with a big key in her hand. She opened the door to a building, half hidden in rubbish and ruins. We entered and found ourselves standing in a beautiful Moorish hall, with lovely, light, entwined bas-reliefs and lace-like filigree carvings on the walls. The ceiling was supported by marble columns, the floor was covered with mosaic. But no one lived here and across the entrance the spider had spun his fine, tough thread, which we had for the moment swept away.

This was the Jewish quarter, once the wealthiest part of the town. Spain's richest Israelites lived here and indeed, according to one legend, they built Toledo. What is certain, however, is that in this place and for a long time they enjoyed many more privileges than anywhere else. They were allowed to build a number of synagogues which look insignificant outside, but inside are glowing with richness and splendour. Two of them still remain as Christian churches, *Nuestra Señora del Tránsito* and *Santa María la Blanca*. The last is the more beautiful, a temple of God with Salomonic splendour. In the filigree, carved walls, which look like fine embroidery, are entwined Hebrew inscriptions, the lovely capitals of the pillars rise into horseshoe arches, light and airy. The temple stands here still but the people of Israel have gone; the buildings around, once so well-appointed, lie in ruins and tenement-like hovels have sprung up in their place. Bright lizards, streaked with gold and other colours, dart in and out of their hiding places in this memory-rich ground. Here the people of Israel lived in their faith and customs, here they were for a time tolerated, but the days of tribulation came and they were shamefully dishonoured and tortured by the Christians. Therefore they turned against them and betrayed them to the Moors, and the Christians revenged themselves against this people in many ways. The ground here has been witness to terror, tears and screams of anguish.

Among the ruins up here we saw a broken granite pillar : upon it in this waste, this desert, sat an old blind beggar, swaddled in his ragged cloak. His features were noble, his white hair hung down over his shoulders. This figure in these surroundings reminded me of a picture I had once seen – the Prophet Jeremiah in the Ruins of Jerusalem. Perhaps the old man had been led up here to pray God to let a little miracle happen, by sending some passer-by to give him a trifle. But it looked as if people never came this way. A great bird of prey flew over our heads, as fearless here as if it were in the wilderness.

Not far from here, in the deserted countryside close by the river Tagus, is Toledo's famous factory where the Damascene blades, swords, daggers and knives are made. It is only a short way out there from the San Martin bridge and one passes more than a few historic and interesting points. Out in the water lie the low remains of old walls which once surrounded the bathing-rooms where Count Julian's lovely daughter, Florinda, sought to refresh herself, playing the naiad in the cooling water, and was seen by Don Rodrigo, King of the Goths. On the little island nearby stood his handsome castle, of which one solitary tower remains. From there he watched the young girl bathing : he took her into his power, but her father avenged this disgrace. He called in the Moors from Africa, who drove out the Goths and their kings.

I know of no place more deserted than the broad carriageway running close up under the old walls of Toledo and no more solitary view than from here. The *campaña* lay as in mourning, the distant, dark mountains looked threatening : everything made one feel grave and sad. I felt as if I were standing by a bier on which some great personage was lying dead. The only sound of life in Toledo comes from the church bells : their ringing is Toledo's heart-beat, pulse and voice.

The sound of one particular bell was strangely ghostly in the still of the night : it had a curious deep clang, hoarse and funereal

– it made me think of the death-bell of the *auto-de-fé* and I imagined that under my window silent phantoms were passing by, the Holy Brotherhood.

By the light of day two of the bells sounded very living and tuneful and they distinctly chimed a name that rang in my ears : one bell sang 'Bianca, Bianca!', the other sang 'Sancho, Sancho!' – this is exactly what they were saying but whom the bells wished to remember by these names I do not know. No one could tell me, but much has happened that is not recorded in history or legend. While I was reflecting on the sound of the bells, it occurred to me that the paving stones in the street echoed with the sound of horses' hooves, as if noble young knights were dashing away on high-spirited steeds, with flowing manes and fine strong legs; the armoury rang with the sound of the heavy iron hammer and lovely women stepped out on to the balconies and sang to the music of the lute.

Of all the bells in Toledo, there is none so great and remarkable as that of the cathedral. It is said that fifteen shoemakers could sit under it and stretch out their cobbler's thread without touching each other. The story goes that the sound of this bell reached right up into heaven, where St Peter thought it was coming from his own church in Rome. But when he saw that this was not the case and that Toledo had the biggest of all bells, he got angry and threw one of his keys down onto the bell, making a crack in it which can still be seen. Were I St Peter I would rather have thrown the key at the head of the person who first invented this story.

The architects say that for age and style the cathedral is one of the most remarkable in the country. The town hall, just across the *plaza*, is a low clumsy building. I do not know to what style it belongs, other than that of ordinary square furniture – it looks like a chest with two drawers, of which the lower has been pulled out. On the *plaza* people were to be seen only when they came out of church. And what grandeur and magnificence there was therein : it was like a petrified woodland arbour, stretching up to the heavens. Arches tower up, at a dizzy height, with filigree, carved, entwined leaves. In the aisles stand altar after altar and a flock of the pious, mostly women in black *mantillas*, kneel here. We saw them bow with deep reverence and make the sign of the Cross as they went past what, to our Protestant eyes, looked like an ordinary paving-stone, preserved behind a thin iron grille, by one of the altars. Upon this stone the Virgin Mary had set her foot when she came down from heaven to the pious faithful of Toledo, thus runs the legend. The organ pealed, there was a sound of chanting and we could hear the church bells as, quietly, we wandered around in the incense-filled aisles and saw the beautiful chapels shining in splendour behind gilded railings. The walls were dazzling with colours and statues. Through the coloured windows the daylight streamed in on marble sarcophagi.

As we left the cathedral the great bell rang out its last peal for the day's services. The air echoed for a long time with the ringing tone and then once again silent, still solitude brooded over town and country: life glided into rest, into the quiet sleep that belongs to vanished days.

XVIII

Burgos

It is only a few hours' journey by train to Madrid from Toledo. Our stay there was prolonged to fourteen days. It was not easy to leave Murillo and Velasquez, it was difficult to say goodbye to the many friendly people I had begun to know, but winter was approaching and there was no heating in our rooms at the hotel. The wind knew to a nicety where to find every little nerve in one's head, throat and chest : it was quite unbearable. If it were not better in Burgos then I would leave Spain with the old year 1862 and go into southern France where the climate was mild and good.

The Swedish Minister, Excellency Bergman, was to the last moment unwearied in his care and attention towards us. When we were due to leave, this elderly man arrived and stayed with us in the cold waiting-room and then in the crowd on the open street until we left. Herr Zobel from Manila and a couple of the young Spanish writers with whom I had made friends also came to say good-bye. I felt quite warm towards Madrid since I had experienced something of the fresh spirit that was abroad there.

The railway line up into France, to Bayonne, is still incomplete in many places : in the beginning we could only go as far as the *Escorial*, the Roskilde of Spain,[1] the mausoleum of Spanish royalty. The silence of death broods over those vaults, over the town and country around.

The place comes to life only when the royal vault is to be opened to receive another coffin. Then the bells ring, trumpets sound, in the great kitchen there is roasting and baking to strengthen the mourners who will go back again to the world of the living.

Philip II built the *Escorial* as his own monument. The red-hot gridiron on which Saint Lawrence was burnt alive by the heathen became a holy symbol and the *Escorial* was planned in this shape. Its courts and buildings form an enormous gridiron. Beneath it rests the Royal Lord, over it whistles the wind in violent gusts from the bare, wild *Guadarrama* mountains, with a sound of moaning and groaning. But there are no mourning spirits in the storm, nor are they heard murmuring through the leaves of the forest – it is through the pages of history that the spirits weep, telling of the dark, cruel deeds of Philip II in his wide dominions over which the sun never set. . . .[2]

In niches, under the high altar, the royal dead lie side by side in black, marble coffins. In the vaults of the palace innumerable cells of monks lie empty and deserted. The vast stone building speaks of greatness and the grave.

It was a dark, gloomy, unpleasant evening when we left the *Escorial*, with a howling wind. Instead of the comfortable railway carriage we were packed into a narrow diligence, which we would have to endure until daybreak. Snow lay round about and the wind blew in at us through the cracks and crevices of the wretched carriage. I wrapped myself in my travelling rug and sat as if I were in a sack, but that way I was less conscious of the piercing wind. A small child with us cried and howled the long night through. There was a snowstorm which made the carriage shake as if it would overturn; a window cracked and the glass fell out – the wind seized its opportunity and the snow drifted in to us. An old *manta* was hung across the gap and we sat in the dark as in a coal-hole, while the carriage swung and jumped about so that there was no thought of sleep, only of broken arms and legs.

At last in San Chidrián we reached the railway line again, but the train was due out only a couple of hours after our arrival. We had to wait in a vast, cold, wooden shed, where everything was in disorder. Here we swallowed some stale, hard bread and a cup of thin chocolate, but we survived.

The signal was given, we crawled into the carriage, the engine puffed and snorted and off we went in the dawn twilight, through the flat landscape. Here there was a vineyard, there a solitary pine tree – it surely was thinking as I was, 'Am I really here in Spain, in one of the warm countries?'

It was nearly twelve o'clock before we got to Burgos. For a long time past we had been able to see the twin towers of the mighty cathedral, but as we got nearer they seemed to sink to their knees, pressed down by the many old city houses round about them.

We took ourselves into the *Fonda de la Rafaela*. The streets were deep in snow and it was bitterly cold, with a wind that penetrated every crack and corner: on the rooms and corridors of the hotel there was a howling draught. We met a number of travellers here from Pamplona and Saragossa, who said that the whole of northern Spain was covered in snow and that wherever one went it would be just as cold and unpleasant. I looked down into the street from my balcony door: people were trudging through deep snow and it was still falling, with large, heavy flakes such as we seldom see at home, even at Christmas. We were frozen. There was no fireplace, but a *brasero* was brought in and over its glowing coals we tried to warm our feet and hands. The two wretched tortoises that Collin had brought from Africa crept right in under the brazier and got their shells heated through.

We wanted to visit the grave of El Cid in the old Benedictine monastery outside the city and we had to see the cathedral, but it was no weather for going out: perhaps it would be better tomorrow.

But one never knows what may happen or will have happened when tomorrow comes. My companion and I were very near to setting out on the long journey to eternity – we were nearly suffocated by charcoal fumes.

I woke up with a feeling of pressure in the pit of my stomach and throbbing in my head. I called to Collin but he lay there even more affected than I. With a great effort I crawled out of bed and, reeling like a drunkard, I reached the balcony door – it was shut fast. I felt desperate and paralysed, but summoning up all my strength I managed somehow to get the door open. The snow drifted in.

We were very unwell for the whole of the next day and were not cheered by better weather. In sleet and slush we stumbled to the cathedral, which is vast, with many splendid tombs and chapels. The memorial chapel of the Velasco family is rich and like a church in itself. The aisles and arches are crowded with marble statues and bas-reliefs, portraits of bishops and archbishops. In a side-chapel there is an old travelling chest or rather trunk hanging up on a wall. According to the legend there should have been two of these historic relics. A ballad recalls that El Cid wanting to borrow money, gave as security to the Jewish moneylenders two chests said to be filled with his silver plate, but the story goes on to say that they were in fact filled with sand, excusing El Cid because he needed the money!

About an hour's journey from Burgos, near to the railway line, is the monastery *Cartuja de Miraflores* and a short walk from there is the old Benedictine monastery, *San Pedro de Cardeña*, where the hero Don Rodrigo Diaz del Cid and his high-minded wife, Jimena, lie buried. We intended to go out there but although we were three days in Burgos we did not manage to visit El Cid's grave. It was not possible to walk or drive there, the snow was too deep.

It was in this district that the famous hero was born in 1026 : he spent part of his life in Burgos where one is shown the remains of his house, and one of the streets bears his name.

The hotel was full of visitors, good-natured Spaniards, friendly and good-humoured young Frenchmen and two travellers whose nationality we could not discover. The lack of heating in the guest rooms and the continuing bad weather brought us all together more often than usual. In the dining-room we gathered in front of the big fireplace, in which logs blazed, and warmed ourselves. Acquaintance was struck up and individual peculiarities soon became obvious.

Among the travellers here we had a man who collected famous teeth and he had a whole 'tooth-album', including a tooth of a bandit who had been executed long ago, a tooth of a well-known singer and, *item*, a tooth of the barber of Zumalacárregui[3] – his celebrities were at least a very mixed lot.

We also had the company of two opposites, two travellers for pleasure for whom travelling was no pleasure. They seemed to have none of the qualities which make for agreeable life together. If one was in humour, the other was grumpy, if one praised something, the other abused it. It was said that they agreed only over one thing and that was that they liked to sleep late into the day. It is true that they let themselves be called each morning, but with the first call they only growled, at the second call they turned over in bed and at the third call they grabbed a stocking – and then fell asleep again with it in their hands.

The same custom prevailed here in Burgos as in Madrid and Toledo : if someone came to call while one was in the middle of dinner, then he would take a chair and sit behind the person he had come to see. Often two or three people would arrive at the same time and there would sit in long-winded conversation, getting in the way of the servants who were trying to wait at table and disturbing the other guests sitting at dinner.

We were already in our third day at Burgos. It was still snowing and the forecast was that all the railways would soon be brought to a standstill. To be forced to stay on here would not be pleasant.

If one wanted to go out and about in the town, either to the gate of Santa Maria with its fine statues or to the ancient cathedral, one had to trudge through the deep snow in one's winter clothes, galoshes on feet and struggling with a large umbrella. It was damp and raw in the streets and in the large, open arcades. One was soon weary of being out in that weather and hurried to get home to the *Fonda Rafaela*, where one either froze in one's own room by the smoking *brasero*, or went down to the dining-room and joined the other good people around the fireplace.

The service in the hotel was in the hands of a couple of servant girls who behaved in a free and easy manner such as we had not found anywhere else in Spain. Had they begun to dance the can-can I should not have been in the least surprised.

At last it lightened a little and the sun broke through, but only for a few minutes. The air was heavy and grey again, snow was falling. If it went on like this we should be forced to celebrate Christmas in El Cid's ancient city. Our young French friends promised us mild and pleasant weather as soon as we had crossed the Pyrenees into their fair fatherland and we must admit that they were right. North of the mountains there were already signs of spring.

XIX

Over the Pyrenees to Biarritz

The clouds dispersed, the sun broke through, the hour of departure had come and we were on our way. The snow lay thrown high on both sides of the railway line. The wind had swept it from the thick ice that covered the ditches and ponds. The old *Cartuja* monastery was almost buried in snowdrifts. Snow, always snow, was our view all the way to Vitoria, but inside the carriage there was all the liveliness of the south, which flowered in speech and song. Only for a short time now should I hear the beautiful, musical language of Spain, which to my ear sounds more sonorous and powerful even than Italian.

We were now in Basque country. The train stopped at Vitoria, a town rich in memories from the wars. During the bloody fighting in the civil war, the army of Queen Christina was defeated here by Zumalacárregui, the popular Carlist hero. The shepherd left his flock, the farmer left his plough; unwearying they risked their lives to bring him intelligence. El Tio, uncle, the soldiers jokingly called him. Here before Vitoria he dashed forward on his white horse; no bullets struck the horse or him, although he was easy enough to recognize in his red basque bonnet, fur jacket and red trousers.*

More recently, though only for a few hours, Vitoria was the focal point for a great scientific gathering. On 18 July 1860 all the astronomers of Europe were assembled here to observe the total eclipse of the sun.

We could see neither sun nor clear sky, only heavy dark clouds: the snow was drifting around, the wind blew and Vitoria hid itself behind a moving white curtain. Every time the carriage

* 27 October 1834. H.C.A.

door was opened we received a shower of great, heavy snow-
flakes. Every traveller who got in shook a whole layer of snow
from himself. The railway line here had not long been opened,
and the train was regarded as something new, something devilish,
by many an old Señora. Every one of them crossed herself when
she took her place and when she heard the whistle of the
signal.

It was evening and quite dark before we reached the tempor-
ary station at Olazagutía where the line ends. A single lamp fed
by train-oil, in the doorway, was the only light for three waiting-
rooms. The floors and corridors were dirty and black from snow
and clayey mud. Here one could be blown through and through
by the wind – if indeed one wanted such a health cure. The wind
and draught were as if one were standing in front of a pair of
bellows. Is this being in Spain, I asked myself, is this what it is
like in a warm country? It was like being at home in the far
North when, at Christmas time, one drives from the highway into
the stables at an inn where the doors stand open and the wind
blows straight through, giving one a taste of snow.

I have no idea what Olazagutía was like, although we had to
stay there for over an hour. Not a building was to be seen in the
darkness which reigned here. A solitary light was shining over
beyond some heaps of snow : someone said there was a restaurant
there. Passengers waded knee-deep in snow to get to it. I stayed
where I was in the hope of finding our luggage and seeing that
it got to the diligence in which we were to travel. There were a
dozen or so vehicles waiting; some were going to Bilbao, others
to Pamplona and yet others to Bayonne. Freight and luggage,
trunks, carpet-bags and hat-boxes glided past me in the snowy
light : they were flung on to the various carriages with a speed
that would have done credit to a juggler. One would be thankful
if in all this muddle and darkness one's own things landed up in
the right vehicle. I had given up all hope.

It was cold and I was hungry : my companion brought me
food and drink, the lifeline of any long journey, which writers
usually tend to ignore. The bread was so old as to be venerable,
the ham was stringy and dry and the wine made one long for

tepid rainwater with a drop of anisette or some other bitter concoction.

Now we were put into the carriage. The horses did not want to go; they were whipped, they were pushed, they were pulled and finally they stepped out. The evening was dark, the night darker; the snow lay high and the carriage lantern shone out over rocks, bushes and deep ravines close to where we were driving – upwards, always upwards.

In the civil war these mountains were the scene of many a bloody guerrilla battle : in these mountains Don Carlos wandered about in rain and snow, at every moment coming upon the watchfires of Queen Christina's troops. Now it was all quiet and peaceful and not once did we see the mounted gendarmes that usually patrol the mountain roads for the safety of travellers. It was safe here even in the dark night. We drove through small sleeping towns, but I did not sleep. A couple of heavily laden diligences, the light of whose lanterns announced their coming a long way ahead, were the only traffic we met. It was still, solitary and winter-cold here, as though we were driving at Christmas time over the mountain ridge between Norway and Sweden and not from Spain into France. We were in the land of the Basques and we could see how hard its climate is in the winter.

At last the road began to descend, the snow drifts became smaller and in the end almost disappeared. We drove into a town; the street lamps were still alight although it was nearly morning. It seemed to be a fair-sized place and looked attractive, with well-built houses and arcades. We were in San Sebastian. The diligence stopped in front of a *fonda* which surprised us by its cleanliness and, I might almost say, elegance. We inspected both the rooms and the kitchen : the chocolate and milk were being heated in clean, polished pans, the whole kitchen shone and the young Basque girl who ruled over it knew how to make her beautiful dark eyes shine too. What they said was easier to understand than the Basque language she spoke : the Basques call it *Eskuara* and scholars say it is derived from Sanskrit – but how many of us Europeans understand that language?

San Sebastian lies on the Bay of Biscay : it is very picturesque with cliffs around it rising steeply up from the deep-green water. We saw the town as the sun rose, painting the clouds fiery red. No one had made any particular mention of this town as being worth a longer visit – which it certainly is. It has all the character of a Spanish town and is in lovely surroundings. In the summer the mountains are covered with wild jasmine and the air is full of its scent. It is to San Sebastian that the French come on short excursions into Spain. Here one is among the original occupants of this part of the country, the strong, tenacious Iberians with their ancient language.

It was a great change and very pleasant surprise to find on the northern side of the Pyrenees a much milder climate than that we had left so recently. Behind us lay the mountains decked with snow; here, on the contrary, the farther north we got, the greener the meadows and fields became and when we reached Irun, the last Spanish town, there were flowers in all the gardens and oranges between the dark leaves of the orange trees.

In Madrid we had had to pay a considerable sum to have our passports stamped with the necessary visas; at Irun a little more tribute money was exacted, but one must have something to grumble about in order not to suggest that everything in Spain was idyllic – and yet that was the main impression and one remembers only the good things.

A long bridge at Behobía forms the frontier : half of it belongs to Spain, the other half to France. The difficulties of travel which I had feared in this foreign, shut-away country, had slipped away as though they had never been. I felt as if I were just coming from a most enjoyable, happy party and was now on my way home, where faithful hearts beat for me, sharing my joys and sorrows.

The maps show us Spain as Miss Europe's head : I had looked into her lovely face and would never forget it. *Dansk* and *Spansk* are rhyming words, as I remember from my childhood days when the Spaniards were in Denmark under Zamora. There is another connection – the Danish folk-hero, Holger Danske, at Ronces-valles in the Spanish Pyrenees fought against the Moors. In Spain he fought with the sword, in Denmark he rallied the spirits of the people.[1]

We were in France. Soon we were in Bayonne, where we were served with ham, a dish for the Nordic gods. A fire in the chimney-piece was our yule log, a wax taper wound around a champagne bottle was lit as a Christmas candle, the cork popped and we drank a toast to Denmark and all our dear ones there: they seemed so near to us and yet we were only a few hours' journey away from Spain and could still see the winter-clad mountains. We would say good-bye to them from Biarritz, the popular health resort near Bayonne on the Bay of Biscay. We drove there in lovely warm sunshine; the trees were in bud as if it were spring. The endless sea stretched out before us, dead calm, but towards the coast, long waves came rolling in like a flock of spouting whales, drenching the sand far in and leaving little pools covered with foam, like a border of lace.

The sea has eaten away large mouthfuls of the steep, porous, rocky coast, forming vast caverns into which it beats and crashes with a sound like the roar of cannon. Along the coast and out in the sea lie great lumps of rock, in wild, chaotic disorder, like strange, gigantic sea-monsters, like petrified prehistoric beasts or the wrecks of sunken ships. The surf breaks high while, far out, the sea looks mirror-calm. When the wind rises, then the waves in the Bay of Biscay rise too, for it is one of the Seven Seas that breaks against this coast, one of the oceans of the world, compared with which Niagara is but a mill-stream. From the cliff top here we saw for the last time the Pyrenees, the lovely mountains of Spain. I was flying home with the other birds of passage to see the beech trees spring into leaf, to hear the cuckoo and all the singing birds, to walk in the tall, fresh, green grass, to hear my mother-tongue and Danish melodies, to see faithful friends, bearing within myself a treasure of memories.

Life itself is the best tale and it has taught me to rejoice.

G

NOTES

CHAPTER I

1 Jonas Collin (1840-1905): only son of Edvard and Henriette and grandson of old Jonas, H.C.A.'s benefactor. Accompanied H.C.A. on trips abroad in 1861, 1862 (to Spain) and 1870. (See Introduction.)

2 'their bells jingling': In a letter written from Spain in 1795, Robert Southey notes: '. . . each mule has sixteen bells: so that we travel more musically and almost as fast as a flying-wagon. There are four reasons why these bells should be worn, two English reasons and two Spanish ones: they may be necessary in a dark night and, where roads are narrow, they give timely warning to other travellers: these are the English reasons. The Spanish motives for using them are, that the mules like the music: and that, as all the bells are marked with a crucifix, the Devil cannot come within hearing of the consecrated peal.'

CHAPTER II

1 *Jeppe paa Bjerget*: a play by Ludvig Holberg, Danish playwright and historian (1684-1754). Jeppe is picked up drunk and wakes to find himself being treated as a nobleman. Cf. the Induction to *The Taming of the Shrew*, and the joke played on Christopher Sly.

2 'Now to Valencia': Weber's work, *Preciosa*, produced in Copenhagen in 1822, was based on Cervantes' exemplary story, *La Gitanella* (The little gypsy girl), and in Act IV a chorus of knights and gypsies sings 'To Valencia, to Valencia – yes and farther, farther away.' One of the songs in H.C.A.'s one-act play, *25 Years Later* (see Introduction) has a verse beginning with this line.

3 *Montserrat* : the sacred mountain of the Catalans, in medieval legend the site of the castle of the Holy Grail. St Ignatius de Loyola was a pilgrim to the monastery there in 1522, and emerged having vowed his life to God. Loyola founded the Society of Jesus, sanctioned by Papal Bull, 1540. He was canonized in 1622.

CHAPTER III

1 'I love the sea' : the opening line of one of H.C.A.'s poems, 1830 (*'Jeg elsker Havet naar det stormer vildt . . .'*).
2 Nyhavn : the picturesque sailors' quarter in Copenhagen. The canal runs from Kongens Nytorv to the harbour. H.C.A. had lodgings there at various times.

CHAPTER IV

1 'the Spaniards in Denmark' : After the attack by the English on Copenhagen in August-September 1807, the Danes signed a treaty with the French (31 October 1807) and a Spanish army under Bernadotte came up through Denmark on their way to Sweden. They did not get there – news came of the rising in France against Napoleon and the Spanish troops mutinied. Before they were returned to France as prisoners, they managed to burn down Koldinghus in Jutland – trying, it is said, to keep themselves warm – and to introduce cigarettes into Denmark.

Zamora was not a person but the name of one of the four Spanish infantry regiments sent to Denmark. (Zamora is a provincial capital and See in S. Leon.)

See also Introduction for H.C.A.'s autobiographical note on this and his two early plays : also reference in Chapter IX.

CHAPTER V

1 'the enchanted garden of Armida' : In Tasso's *La Gerusalemme Libertata* (1575), Armida's garden charms the knights from their duty.

CHAPTER VI

1 Prudentius: Aurelius Clemens, 348 - *c.* 405 AD. Born in Spain, he was the foremost poet of the Early Church, and a contemporary of Ambrose, Augustine and Jerome. H.C.A. is thinking of the funeral hymn :

> *Med sorgen og klagen hold maade,*
> *Du mindes den hellige daab,*
> *Himmerigs bord af Guds naade!*
> *Tilegn dig Guds herligheds haab!*

CHAPTER VII

1 'Galley slaves' : George Borrow (*The Bible in Spain*) refers to the galleys at Málaga. Lt. Col. Napier in 1838 saw some 1,500 or 2,000 such convicts there.

2 'Arion' : According to legend, Arion, in *c.* 625 BC, was returning from a song-contest and threw himself into the sea to avoid being murdered by the sailors who wanted to steal his trophies. He was rescued by the song-loving dolphins who had gathered round the ship to hear him play the cithara. (Herodotus)

CHAPTER VIII

1 'a half-orange' : This is the *media naranja* – the accepted technical term for the cupola form in Spanish architecture.

2 the Ommayad Caliphs : the first Arabian Caliph dynasty founded in 661 : they established an independent Caliphate at Córdoba in 756 which lasted until 1031. (See also Chapter XIII.)

3 The chestnut seller : H.C.A.'s verse about the gypsy girl selling chestnuts (omitted from our translation) was used as the text – and the pretext – for a caricature of him in the Danish student magazine *Svœrmere* in April 1863. (See illustration and Introduction.) The verse, literally translated, reads :

By the wall of the house was a hedge of geraniums,
Where she sat on the marble steps,
So young, so lovely, selling chestnuts.
There she sat with a flower in her hair, and bare legs,
She gazed at one with two lovely eyes.
If one were not made of ice, one would at once turn into
                                        a Spaniard.

4 Washington Irving: 1783-1859. American writer and diplomat, he was on the staff of the US Embassy in Spain, 1826-29, and was US Minister there, 1842-46. He stayed in the *Alhambra* in 1829 and wrote a long account of the place and its legends, with photographs and engravings which show it very much as H.C.A. must have seen it.

5 Málaga's Protestant Cemetery: founded in 1829 by the then British Consul, William Mark. Before that time, Protestants dying in Spain were buried below low-water mark or out at sea – as they were, too, in e.g. Madeira. Richard Ford gives a more detailed description (*Gatherings from Spain*).

CHAPTER IX

1 Lindaraja: a Moorish Princess in the romances and legends of the Moors' last days in Granada.

2 F.W. Hackländer: His book, *Ein Winter in Spanien* (1855), was one of those used by H.C.A. in preparation for and on his journey. (See Introduction.)

3 The Barracks of the Córdoba Regiment: former *Castillo de Bibataubin*, destroyed in the Civil War. They were built on the pattern of Potsdam and the soldiers' statues were in the uniform of the time of Frederick the Great. (See Sacheverell Sitwell, *Spain*.)

4 'Denmark, where the Spaniards had been': See Chapter IV, note 1.

5 Bournonville, August (1805-1879): choreographer, created thirty-six Ballets and *divertissements*, several of which are still in the repertoire of the Royal Danish Ballet.

6 *Fonda de los Siete Suelos*: In his Journal for 17 October 1863 Andersen says: 'The hotel takes its name from the old tower nearby

which is part of the fortress wall of the *Alhambra*, the *Torre de los Siete Suelos* (i.e. the tower of the seven storeys).'

7 Salvator Rosa: Neapolitan painter, d. 1673, noted for rather wild and gloomy pictures – landscapes with brigand-like figures. His 'Saul and the Witch of Endor' is in the Louvre.

8 'a famous English photographer': Charles Clifford was Court Photographer to Queen Isabella II, who presented albums of his photographs to her friends. There is a bound album in the *Alhambra* Library of the pictures he took during her State Visit to Andalucia and Murcia during September-October 1862, and collections of his work are known to be in the Royal Palace in Madrid and in the Art Museum in Gothenburg. Unfortunately, these are not catalogued. Clifford died in Madrid on 1 January 1863 and is buried in the British Cemetery there.

CHAPTER X

1 the Nordstjerne: the Swedish Order of the North Star: H.C.A. received it in 1848 – with a black ribbon since it was on the day of the funeral of King Christian VIII. He went to Sweden and was received in audience by King Oscar I on 1 June 1849 in order to say thank you. At this time (in 1862) H.C.A. had: the Prussian Red Eagle, the White Falcon of Saxe-Weimar, the Order of Maximilian and the Knight Cross of Dannebrog.

2 Oehlenschläger, Adam (1779-1850): Danish poet and play-wright, was made a knight of Nordstjernen in 1829 and a Commander in 1840. (See *A Visit to Portugal 1866*, Chapter III, note 16.) The reference is probably to the reception by the critics of H.C.A.'s play, *Ahasverus*, in 1847. Oehlenschläger said to him: 'The Northern Star never goes down, you shall bear it when I am gone.'

3 Sir John Drummond Hay: 1816-1893. Chargé d'Affaires and Consul-General in Morocco (Minister Plenipotentiary, 1872), PC, KCB, GCMG. He served in Constantinople 1840 and succeeded his father in Morocco in 1845. He married Annette, daughter of J.A.H. Carstensen, the Danish Consul-General in Tangier, whom he also succeeded as representative of Denmark. He had two daughters,

Louisa (1849-1902), m. John Brooks, and Alice (1851-1940) who was
born in Copenhagen and died in Vallø, Denmark.

In 1844 Drummond Hay had negotiated with the Sultan of
Morocco on behalf of Sweden and Denmark for the ending of their
annual payment to the Sultan for protection against piracy : he was
offered their 'Orders' as a reward which, as a diplomat, he had to
refuse.

H.C.A. met Drummond Hay again in Copenhagen in 1863 and
read Chapter XI to him. H.C.A.'s description of the house Revens-
rock and his subsequent letters to Lady Drummond Hay are quoted
in the Memoir of Sir John Drummond Hay by his daughter Louisa
(see Chapter XI, note 3).

4 *Calla* : the arum lily. It has not been possible precisely to identify
the flower that H.C.A. saw in Gibraltar and Tangier. The *datura
metel* is certainly white and like a lily in shape, but it does not
change colour – it can however be slightly rose-coloured. The
hibiscus mutabilis has white flowers which turn pink and they last
only one day – but they are really not much like the *Calla*.

CHAPTER XI

1 Mr Green : As Sir William Kirby Green, he succeeded Drummond Hay as Minister to the Court of Morocco in 1886.

2 'The Marsh-King's Daughter' : *Dyndkongens Datter*, translated
by Jules Jürgensen in *Fantasies Danoises, Contes d'Andersen*
(Geneva, 1861).

3 Mahmud II (1785-1839) : The 'present Sultan' was Abd-el-Aziz,
s. of Mahmud II. This story is told in the Memoir of Sir John
Drummond Hay by his daughter Louisa (L.A.E. Brooks); the dwarf
is there supposed to have said : 'Can a bramble entwine the top of
the lofty cypress?'

Drummond Hay met the 'sultana' in Constantinople and there
bought a copy of the portrait : he gave it to Lady Ponsonby, the
wife of the Ambassador, as a farewell present (according to his
daughter's Memoir). It has not been possible to establish whether
this picture is still in the possession of the Ponsonby family.

4 'one of their princesses' : Catherine of Braganza, who married

Charles II in 1662, bringing with her as dowry Tangier and Bombay. Tangier was held by England only until 1684.
5 'the first verse of *Genesis* in Hebrew' : Hebrew was taught in Danish grammar schools until 1871.

CHAPTER XII

1 'a really Spanish story' : There are a dozen or so words in Danish with the prefix 'Spanish' (*Spansk*) which they mostly do not carry over into English : the point, in this particular context, is therefore lost in direct literal translation. Among the objects mentioned in the original text by H.C.A. – which he might be expected to write about – are : *Spansk peber* (cayenne), *Spanskrør* (cane), *Spanskgrønt* (verdigris), *Spanske fluer* (the Spanish fly, *cantharis*, which was dried and used for raising blisters and as an aphrodisiac, etc.), and *Spanske kappe* (Spanish cape or cloak). This last was a barrel used as a form of punishment : the victim stood in it with his arms, legs and head through holes (cf. the stocks and pillory). Holberg (see Chapter II, note 1) mentions this in one of his plays and also uses the expression *Spanskulere* or *Gaa og se Spansk ud* – defined as 'to strut about'. The last known example of this 'cape' in Denmark was burnt there in 1795, but it had long since gone out of use.

In the event, H.C.A. did not make use of any of these objects or topics in the work that came out of his visit to Spain (see Introduction). He mentions the assonance of *Dansk/Spansk* at the end of the book (see Chapter XIX and note 2).
2 'four boards await us all' : a quotation from a hymn by Dorothea Engelbretsdatter, 1634-1716. Cf. *Hamlet*, 5, i : 'Has this fellow no feeling of business that he sings at grave-making?' 'Custom hath made it in him a property of easiness.'

CHAPTER XIII

1 Rossini's *Barber of Seville* was first produced in 1816. At the time of H.C.A.'s visit there were already no less than eight well-known operas with a Spanish setting. Verdi's *La Forza del Destino*

had its première on 10 November 1862 (see Chapter XVI, note 4) :
still to come were *Don Carlos* (1867) and Bizet's *Carmen* (1875).
2 John Phillip, R.A. (1817-1867): After a visit to Seville he
specialized in Spanish folk scenes and became known as 'Spanish
Phillip' or 'Phillip of Spain'. He made some copies of Velasquez
pictures which were described as excellent : one, of 'The Infanta' –
a detail of *'Las Meninas'* (see illustration) – was bought by the
Royal Academy and another, 'The Surrender of Breda', by the
National Gallery of Scotland. He was commissioned by Queen
Victoria to paint the official picture of the wedding of the Princess
Royal in 1858 and produced many highland scenes, including one
of the Queen and Prince Consort at the Highland Games. According
to his Journal, H.C.A. visited Phillip in his studio on 20 November,
where the artist was painting a Spanish girl. They exchanged personal photographs and Phillip gave H.C.A. a photograph of one of
his Spanish paintings – unfortunately it does not appear to have
survived in any of the Andersen Collections.

Egron Sellif Lundgren (1815-1875) lived for some time in London : with Phillip he did the illustrations for Henry Blackburn's
Travelling in Spain at the Present Day (1866), some of which were
used in the same author's *A Thousand Miles Towards the Sun*
(London, 1892).
3 *La Caridad* : built in 1661-1664 and founded by Don Miguel de
Mañara, whose portrait, sword and death mask are there, not by
Don Juan Tenorio. H.C.A. is right in saying that the two traditions
are mixed.
4 The Tobacco factory was, of course, the setting for *Carmen* (see
note 1 above).

CHAPTER XIV

1 'We believe, we all believe in God. . . .' : the Lutheran version
of the Creed.

CHAPTER XV

1 Schiller's *Don Carlos* (on which Verdi's opera was based) was

translated into Danish in 1830 by Rahbek. For Philip II and his 'happy days at Aranjuez' see also Chapter XVII.

CHAPTER XVI

1   Opera in Madrid : H.C.A. saw there *Il Trovatore*, *Lucia di Lammermoor* and two Donizetti operas. In his Journal for 10 December he says that at *Lucia* he saw the Queen wearing 'light blue silk and red roses in her hair'.

Signora Anne Caroline de la Grange (b. 1825) was a French coloratura singer. Elsewhere H.C.A. compares her with Jenny Lind.

2   Velasquez, Diego v. de Silva (1599-1660) : H.C.A. is clearly describing the famous '*Las Meninas*' (see Chapter XIII, note 2). According to tradition, Philip IV (1621-1665) himself painted in the ribbon of an Order on a Velasquez self-portrait, which the artist had deliberately omitted.

3   Thorvaldsen, Bertel (1770-1844) : famous Danish sculptor whom H.C.A. knew in Rome. The 'Guardian Angel' bas-rélief is one of a series now in the Cathedral (*Vor Frue Kirke*) in Copenhagen.

4   Verdi had in fact already completed the music for *La Forza del Destino* (to de Rivas's libretto) : the opera had its première in St Petersburg on 10 November 1862 while H.C.A. was in Spain.

CHAPTER XVII

1   Jacob Kornerup (1825-1913) : Danish painter of architecture and archaeologist. H.C.A. saw his Spanish pictures before his journey but apparently only saw his book, *Skildringer fra Spanien i 1860*, after his return (noted in his Journal for 9 August 1863).

CHAPTER XVIII

1   'the Roskilde of Spain' : Roskilde Cathedral is the mausoleum of the Danish sovereigns. There seems here to be an echo of the Spanish saying : '*Los muertos en la huesa y los vivos a la mesa*' – 'the dead in their grave, the quick to dinner', quoted by Richard Ford.

2 'dominions over which the sun never sets' : This phrase was attributed originally to the Emperor Charles V (Charles I of Spain, 1500-1558, grandson of Ferdinand and Isabella and father of Philip II). Schiller gives it to Philip II in his *Don Carlos.*

3 Zumalacárregui, Tomas (1788-1835) : Basque General and Carlist leader : fell at the siege of Bilbao. (See also Chapter XIX, para. 2.)

CHAPTER XIX

1 Holger Danske : legendary Danish hero who fought at the Battle of Roncesvalles, 778. In the *Song of Roland* he is Ogier le Danois – and may indeed have been Ogier l'Ardennois. The French poem was used as the basis for *Holger Danskes Krønike* (1534) by Christian Pedersen. Holger Danske sits today in the castle of Kronborg at Helsingør, from whence he will come to succour Denmark in her hour of need. H.C.A. wrote a story about the Holger Danske legend (see Chapter XVI). For a note on the *Spansk* words in Danish, see Chapter XII, note 1.

SELECTED BIBLIOGRAPHY

1

H.C. Andersen

I Spanien, ed H.C. Paludan (*Romaner og
Rejseskildringer*, Volume VII : *Det Danske
Sprog – og Litteraturselskab*, under the
direction of H. Topsøe-Jensen). Copenhagen:
Gyldendal, 1944.
I Spanien, with illustrations by Hans
Bendix. Copenhagen : Carit Andersens
Forlag, 1971.
Dagbøger 1861-63, Volume V, ed. Tue Gad
and Kirsten Weber : *Det Danske Sprog – og
Litteraturselskab* under the direction of Kare
Olsen and H. Topsøe-Jensen. Copenhagen :
G.E.C. Gads Forlag, 1971.
Mit Eget Eventyr Uden Digtning, ed. H.
Topsøe-Jensen. Copenhagen : Hans Reitzel,
1959.
*Brevveksling med Edvard og Henriette
Collin*, ed. H. Topsøe-Jensen. Copenhagen :
Levin and Munksgaard, 1933-37.
*Breve til Therese og Martin Henriques
1860-75*, ed. H. Topsøe-Jensen. Copenhagen:
H. Hagerup, 1932.

2

Aase and Carl
Luplau Janssen

'Hans Christian Andersen i Granada',
Oxenvad. Odense, 1961.
Anderseniana, Vol. IV, No. 2, ed. Niels

Reginald Spink

Hans Christian Andersen and His World.
London : Thames and Hudson, 1972.

Signe Toksvig

Life of Hans Christian Andersen. London :
Macmillan, 1934 (Danish edition, Copenhagen : Hernovs Forlag, 1970).

3

William Atkinson

A History of Spain and Portugal. London :
Pelican Books, 1960.

George Borrow

The Bible in Spain. London : Everyman's
Library, Dent, 1961.

Mary Fitton

Málaga: the biography of a city. London :
Allen and Unwin, 1971.

Richard Ford

Gatherings from Spain (from *A Handbook
to Spain, 1845*). London : Everyman's
Library, Dent, 1970.

Marjorie Grice-
Hutchinson

The English Cemetery at Málaga. The
author, 1964.

Washington Irving

The Alhambra. London and New York :
G.P. Putnam and Sons, 1851.

Rose Macaulay

Fabled Shore. London : Hamish Hamilton,
1949-73.

H.V. Morton

A Stranger in Spain. London : Methuen,
1955.

Oleg Polunin and
Anthony Huxley

Flowers of the Mediterranean. London :
Chatto and Windus, 1965.

Felipe Torroba Ber-
naldo de Quirós

The Spanish Jews. Madrid, 1972.

Sacheverell Sitwell

Spain. London : Batsford, 1950.

Robert Southey

*Letters written during a Short Residence in
Spain and Portugal, 1795.* London : Long-
man and Rees, 1799.

Honor Tracy

Spanish Leaves. London : Methuen, 1964.

4
L.A.E. Brooks
(Louisa Drummond
Hay)

*A Memoir of Sir John Drummond Hay,
KCB, GCMG.* London : John Murray, 1896.

Graham H. Stuart

The International City of Tangier.
California : Stanford University Press, 1955.